...ives scattered
...o Nepal to rural
...t to life through 17
...uccesses of ordinary

...r life, whether in
...n their future and
...ely diverse paths,
...hey worked toward
...aps begin writing

. . .

...t of time we have in
...blind spots that keep
...a pathway or way of
...ring readers to take
...nge to their lives and

...s *of Fine Art Photography*
...lery owner, and
...ctor at Parsons
...ed Nations Alliance
...of State on cultural
...consultant working with
...nd not for profits.

...g software executives
...oft, he worked directly
...la. He has co-created and
...s Apple, Amazon, Meta,
...ce, Azure, and xBox.
...nies around the world.

...asing & Beauty
PUBLISHING
...hasingbeautypublishing.com

Twenty One Summers

THOMAS WERNER & DERRICK CONNELL

Twenty One Summers

Become

THO...

TWENTY ONE SUMMERS

TWENTY ONE SUMMERS

Time is Precious, So Are Your Dreams
Become Who You Are Meant to Be

Thomas Werner and Derrick Connell

Copyright © 2026 Thomas Werner and Derrick Connell

All rights reserved.

No part of this book may be reproduced, stored in a retrieval system, or transmitted in any form or by any means—electronic, mechanical, photocopying, recording, or otherwise—without the prior written permission of the author, except for brief quotations used in reviews or scholarly works.

Published by
Chasing Beauty Publishing
1212 North Summit Drive
Santa Fe, New Mexico 87501
www.chasingbeautypublishing.com

ISBN (paperback): 979-8-9943836-0-5
ISBN (eBook): 979-8-9943836-1-2

Printed in the United States of America

First edition 2026

Cover design: Kirsti Itameri
Interior design and typesetting: Maria Giovanna Brauzzi

CONTENTS

ACKNOWLEDGMENTS

A Special Thank You

To Debbie and Cira, for your support and understanding throughout the project

Our Deep Appreciation

To Mike for his guidance and mentorship, and to Leah for her incredible research and outreach

Thank You

Faith and Veronica for all of your help. To Mardi for her work on the website, Maria for typesetting the book, and Kirsti for the extraordinary cover and design

Our Gratitude

To the friends, family, and colleagues who offered encouragement throughout this process. Thank you for believing in the book and helping make it a reality

Twenty One Summers would not be possible without the stories that bring the book to life and inspire us to achieve. The wisdom and insight provided by those who took time out of their busy schedules to sit down for an interview is priceless. Thank you for your kindness and generosity. Your vision, knowledge, and experience are invaluable and will help many

ABOUT THE AUTHORS

Thomas Werner

Thomas is the author of the books *The Business of Fine Art Photography*, Routledge, New York, and *The Fashion Image* for Bloomsbury Publishing, London. He is also an Editor at Large for IRKmagazine, a Paris based print publication and website, Board Member for the Santa Fe's CENTER for Photographic Art, and past Photography Program Director at Parsons School of Design in New York. He is the former owner of Thomas Werner Gallery in Manhattan's Chelsea Art District, and a former National Board Member and New York Chapter President for the American Society of Media Photographers, as well as a former Advisory Board Member for Ithaca College's Executive Education Program, contributor to Adobe's Lightroom Academy, and a photography consultant for COACH, among others. As an exhibiting artist, Thomas was represented by galleries in New York and Los Angeles, and his work reviewed in The New Yorker Magazine.

Werner led a team developing a media and literacy website for the United Nations Alliance of Civilizations/ UNESCO and was a recurring instructor for the United Nations Education First Summer School. From 2005 to 2019, he worked with the United States Department of

State on cultural projects in Russia partnering with 32 cultural, educational, and governmental organizations to develop projects in 29 cities. Partners have included: The State Hermitage Museum, the National Center of Contemporary Art, Perm Regional Government, The Moscow Biennale for Young Art, National Centre of Photography for the Russian Federation, The Central State Archive of Film, Photographic and Phonographic Documents, The Moscow Biennale, and others. His private collection of Russian photographs and artifacts have been exhibited internationally.

Currently a creative consultant, Thomas works one on one with creatives, businesses, cultural institutions, and not for profits, helping them with career development, team management, innovation, education, and the development of effective communication across multiple media platforms.

IG @Thomaswernerprojects

www.Thomaswernerprojects.com

Derrick Connell

Derrick is one of the world's leading software executives in the fields of Search and AI. He is the holder of seven US Patents approved and nine US Patents pending, including one with Bill Gates and others with several of the world's leading information retrieval computer scientists. Derrick has led global product and engineering teams comprised of 4,000 of the world's best product managers, machine learning scientists, software developers and designers, tasked with delivering global products and services directly to consumers via partners such as Apple, Amazon, Meta, Twitter and Yahoo, or through Microsoft products such as Windows, Office, Azure and Xbox. He has also co-created products with companies such as Apple with the integration of Microsoft's core AI service as part of Siri, Facebook with the co-development of a social search service, as well as collaborations with Amazon.

He was a founding member of the team that created the Bing search engine in 2009, the technology powers Microsoft's search engine. Derrick also led the development of many new Search and AI features in Microsoft Windows, Office, and Xbox. Over the course of his career at Microsoft he has worked directly with all three of the company's CEOs, Bill Gates, Steve Ballmer, and Satya Nadella. From 2011 to 2020, he was the corporate vice president for Microsoft's Search and AI business and one of the leading advisors to the current CEO Satya Nadella on the company's AI strategy. During this period he created a profitable multi-billion dollar business for the company.

Derrick currently works as an advisor to many companies around the world, including the UK-based Ocado, advising them on their technology investments in robotics and AI. He also advises innovation start-ups in the field of mixed reality, helping them deliver on their vision of the Metaverse and AI to deliver products across multiple fields. One company, Mesmerise, recently launched a joint venture with the Mayo Clinic.

IG @Derrick_Connell

Chapter One

Twenty One Summers

It was one o'clock on a fall afternoon in New York. I was standing at the front of an auditorium filled with college students at the start of the semester. Looking out at them I wondered about their dreams, what they imagined their lives would be like, what career paths they would take, and why they chose the majors that they were in. Knowing my own expectations while in school and the unexpected and unimaginable path my life has taken, it seemed time to check in, so I began. Stepping up to the edge of the stage I asked what their average age was. After some serious debate they decided on twenty two as opposed to twenty one. Next, I asked how long they thought they would live and suggested eighty, as the average life expectancy in the United States is seventy five years old for a man and eighty for a woman. Eighty, they argued, was too young so we settled on eighty two.

That gave them all sixty years to accomplish everything they desired in life. A lifetime of time where everything was possible. In school years that was sixty summers, as summers were free and the time to explore. If they attempted or accomplished one thing in each of those summers, they were going to be able to do sixty things in their life between that day in class and when they died.

They agreed when I said that last dozen years of life might not allow for more physically demanding travel or goals, which meant they had forty eight summers to achieve their goals and dreams. Then I pointed out that if they had children the first thirteen years of their child's life would limit the things they could do, which left them with thirty five summers. Thirty five things that they could accomplish from that day onward. At that point people became restless and some said the conversation wasn't fair, but the truth was that there were going to be at least seven years when they would not be able to take on their goals in the same way due to their health or finances, and seven more when taking care of a family member or other issues were going to keep each of them from exploring, learning, and doing as they wished, which left Twenty One Summers. If they did one thing each summer, and most of them would not, they could achieve twenty one things between that day and the day they passed.

I then asked why they were in my class, why they were attending that school, why they had chosen the majors they were in, and what they really wanted to do with their lives. The goal was not to make them feel as if they had little time left, nor to diminish family, children, and careers, some of life's most important achievements, but to make them question the choices that they were making, to think about what their priorities were, and to be aware of the lives they were often unconsciously choosing.

The goal was to make them cognizant of how precious your dreams and desires are and to help them understand that you aren't just choosing a partner, a career, or city to live in, you are choosing a lifestyle.

Time slips away from us. Sometimes in large chunks and other times in small pieces. We become wrapped up in day to day responsibilities and are unaware of how quickly life moves past us. One moment it seems like we have forever and then all of a sudden ten summers have passed and we wonder what happened, asking ourselves when we will have the chance to do the things we love.

Whether it is after seventeen years of school, a divorce, the loss of a loved one, a planned or unplanned career change, a friendship that ends, retirement, or just an average day in our lives, there are times when we ask ourselves who we are, what have we been doing with our lives, and what will we become. During these moments, it is essential to be aware of the forces that are affecting our decision making, whether we are making life changing choices or the small daily decisions that may ultimately impact our entire lives. It is time to be aware of what we call our Blind Spots. The phrase 'blind spot' was first used by Edme Mariotte to describe a loss of vision, with the earliest documentation in the 1660s. In psychology, the phrase can be traced back to Sigmund Freud and Carl Jung, but the concept has been explored and written about by researchers ever since. For us, Blind Spots are ways of thinking, habits and influences at work in your life, often without you knowing it, that keep you from growing, changing, and achieving your goals big and small. They are obstacles that will keep you from fulfilling your Twenty One Summers.

Before diving into the rest of the book, take a moment and sit down by yourself or with your family, friends, or book club and come up with your own Twenty One Summers. This is a list of things to do, a combination of your dreams, desires, who you aspire to be, goals you would like to achieve, the lifestyle you would like to live, and the changes that you would like to make in yourself or your life. Don't limit yourself, write down whatever comes to mind. As you do so consider which is your most important goal, or goals, your Core Twenty One. You don't need to have an answer for that yet, but we do want you to begin thinking about it.

After each chapter take a little time to reflect on the Blind Spot described or the individuals' stories you've read and think about how they might relate to your own life. After you do, revisit your list and update your Twenty One Summers. Watch how your Summers evolve and your goals change as you start to recognize and overcome your Blind Spots, taking steps toward a more fulfilling life.

Remember, Twenty One Summers is an idea, a guidebook, a pathway, or way of living, your list may not have exactly twenty one items, it may have twelve, ten, or five. If you are about to graduate you have a lifetime to achieve your Twenty One, and if you are retiring you may have exactly Twenty One Summers left to make life amazing in new ways. You may be mid-life, mid-career, or empty nesting, and wondering how you ended up where you are, what is next, and whether positive change is possible. Or you might want to make one or two specific things happen in your life, if so, then focus on those goals. Not to worry if you aren't able to make a list yet, we will address that too. Some of the most successful people Derrick and I know have struggled to define their first Twenty One. Yours will emerge as you move through the book.

The book itself should be viewed in its entirety, as each step unfolds, building on those that precede it, much like the process for understanding, identifying, and engaging your Twenty One Summers. Every chapter is filled with a diverse group of stories that illustrate our challenges and successes, providing insight into how others have overcome obstacles and reached their goals. Blind Spots are also addressed throughout, allowing us to look at larger and more comprehensive solutions with each chapter.

Ultimately, Twenty One Summers is a book about you, your life, and your desire to create positive change for yourself or others. It is about what is holding you back and how to move past those challenges to a happier and more fulfilling place in life. As you define your Twenty One Summers and engage potential Blind Spots we want you to keep one thing in mind. *Let Life Treat You Well.* You deserve it.

Chapter Two

Who Am I,
Who Am I Supposed To Be,
Who Can I Be

It was the morning after graduating from the University of Wisconsin in Madison. The papers were done, presentations given, and capstone experiences complete. There were last nights out with people from class and a party for closest friends. Family had driven in for the day to celebrate, this was an event. My parents were proud as I was the first person from our family to graduate from college. After the ceremony, my father shook my hand. It was the first time that I saw him cry and that meant the world to me, more than the degree. After the ceremony we all went out for a formal dinner and then later that evening everyone slowly left for home.

The next morning there I was, alone in my apartment. Nobody had told me about this part, when the excitement is over and it is just you sitting in inescapable silence needing to decide what it is next. Seventeen years of being known as a student were over and it was time to start a new life, my life. The world was open to me. Everything seemed possible, and nothing seemed possible.

I took a deep breath and realized that even though I didn't know exactly where I was going in life I had to get moving, because if I didn't I was going to be in that little apartment in Madison, Wisconsin for a long time. It was time to start living my Twenty One Summers, which unbeknownst to me were going to take me places that twenty four year old Thomas could not begin to imagine.

This is a moment that I have lived in different variations throughout my life, and so have you. Each time an occasion like this occurs it comes down to the same decision, take a breath, let go of pre-existing definitions and limitations, and begin moving forward. It is time to reboot, to reconsider, to evolve. The other choice that morning in Madison was to stay exactly where I was, and that was not an option.

During each of those moments in life, there were a series of very well defined Blind Spots at work that I did not completely understand. Blind Spots inhibit and deceive, costing you valuable time and opportunities. Opportunities that may lead to achieving your Twenty One Summers. We will discuss Blind Spots throughout the book, but the first, *Who Am I*, had been in effect for virtually my entire life. Since the age of five I had been defined as a student, my friends were students, and the majority of the choices that I had made were centered around education and activities associated with it. Now I was being asked to let go of a central part of the way I defined myself and my identity to the world. The idea was daunting.

The second Blind Spot at work after graduation was *Who Am I Supposed To Be*. Since the start of kindergarten everything I had learned pointed toward graduation and the moment I would step into the world and fulfill my potential. To be honest, I didn't have a clear vision of who I was supposed to be after graduation or how I was going to get there. On a larger scale I wondered if I had the necessary skills to get a good job, what my career would be like, if I would be successful, where I was going to live, if I was going to meet someone and fall in love, get married, and have a family. The questions seemed endless. My parents had expectations for me post-graduation, as did family and friends, and despite their love, support, and understanding, I felt a great responsibility to please them and succeed in the ways they imagined. Not to mention my own expectations for my life and career. All of our expectations were well meant, but in the end, they were limiting. The questions I had regarding *Who Am I Supposed To Be* were not all of my own making, nor are the questions you may have regarding who you should or want to be.

Derrick and I both grew up in small rural working class towns. We were lucky as we came from homes where people worked hard and family was important. We were inspired to be curious and to question, but were expected to come up with informed answers and not just opinions. Our parents cared about education and its role as a stepping stone to a potential future, yet neither of us understood how to connect academics and what we were learning with a potential career path.

Derrick lived with his mother, father and three brothers in Trim, Ireland, a small town just outside of Dublin. It was surrounded by farms with the town hub existing to support family owned businesses and the local tourist trade. His father was a self-made businessman with little formal education who became the main milk distributor and his mother a skilled seamstress. Life was simple in both our towns, but there were expectations for each of us. My parents, sister, and I lived in a growing farm and commuter community filled with forests and freedom just outside of Milwaukee, Wisconsin. My father worked in a local factory and my mother was the secretary at a grade school and a church. Life was good and hard work was valued, as was putting in the time and effort necessary to move ahead in life.

Both of our parents worked to give us the opportunity to attend school and to build a better life than they had lived. Their sacrifices were beautiful and honorable but they also created the weight of expectation. There is nothing wrong with having expectations, they are essential to overcoming your Blind Spots, but it is important to understand where those expectations come from and how they are holding you back. For each of us a college degree was supposed to be the key to life. Yet a few months after graduating I found myself working at a movie theater in Los Angeles wearing polyester pants and a dickey, asking people if they would like butter on their popcorn. It was a humbling experience. The degree that I thought was the passport to my future had not delivered the job that I had envisioned. Both my and my family's expectations and assumptions were proven untrue. But how could that be? I had done everything that was expected of me. It would have been easy to be angry and bitter, but that would not have changed anything. It wasn't until I could begin to let go of the first two Blind Spots, *Who Am I* and *Who Am I Supposed To Be*, that my life began to change.

Derrick graduated with a degree in computer science, a new field that people at the time knew little about. It was 1989, Microsoft was founded in 1975 and the first prototype of an Apple computer was developed in 1976, so home computers were rare. As Derrick noted, "When I stood in the middle of our town and looked at the options for a career I didn't see a lot that attracted me. On the left side of main street were jobs like banking, legal, dentist, clothing store owner, or baking. On the right side was a pub, hotel, farming supply company, and the equestrian shop. There was a natural pressure to select one of these jobs. At some point in our teens a zinc mine opened in the nearby town. That created a new set of possibilities for electricians, miners, drivers, and some other mining work. We all went to a mandatory aptitude test for this company and I didn't do very well. My brother did and got his first gig as a trainee electrician in the mines. He was a DIY kind of guy and still is. I could barely change a lightbulb." Derrick ended up working at a small tech start-up in London that oftentimes wouldn't pay him. Bartending weekends to pay his rent and coding late into the night he would fall asleep on the floor by his desk and be woken up with a kick each morning with his bosses asking why he wasn't working harder.

These were hardly glamorous beginnings, but neither of our experiences held us back. In the end, *Who Am I* was neither defined by the first jobs we had out of college, nor solely by our upbringing. We both took a risk by leaving the familiarity of our hometown and were on our way to taking on the third Blind Spot *Who Can I Be.*

Who Can I Be was certainly at work that morning in Madison. I knew that I was supposed to get a job, work hard, have a family, and one day purchase a nice house. There were jobs out there, but I wasn't sure which ones were a good fit for me or my degree. Many required more years of experience than I had, others were in places that I did not want to live. Looking back there was a long list of careers that I didn't even know existed. Yet I believed that hard work and hope would prevail, so I loaded everything I owned into my car and drove to California. Like the students in my class in New York, Derrick and I had our entire lives ahead of us. It was time to begin working toward possibilities known and unknown, time to start living our Twenty One Summers and finding out what our *Who Am I* and *Who Can I Be* really were.

Your self-identity begins to develop at birth; it is a compilation of the environments that you live in, the daily interactions that you have with the world, your successes and challenges, and the people around you who influence you and your life. A large part of your self-identity comes from the belief systems that you grow up in, whether they are those of your family, friends, colleagues, country, or community. As children we internalize the beliefs of those around us as that is often the only way we know how to navigate the world. We decide what is right and wrong and what possibilities are available to us based on our environment and the information and feedback we receive from others.

School also plays an important role in defining our expectations and our *Who Am I, Who Am I Supposed To Be* and *Who Can I Be*. For Derrick and I that was, who is an artist and who is a scientist or technician? These two roles are often thought of as separate, either you are creative or logical, practical, and more scientific. Students are frequently placed in one group or another by educators, counselors, and programs that make these decisions based on a handful of tests, classes, assumptions, or curriculum. Doing so ignores the range of knowledge that a student may possess and more importantly the crossover between art, science, and technology that Derrick and I have lived on a daily basis. A teacher or friend saying that you are not good at science or not talented as an artist can affect your choices for the rest of your life. I couldn't draw, wasn't a painter, and didn't like making sculpture, so wasn't considered an artist at my high school. Photography had not entered my life at the time as I didn't think that it was an appropriate career choice. *Who Am I* got in the way as well as I didn't dress or act like the people who were in the art classes at school. They had different interests and talked about things that I wasn't involved in. My understanding of what it meant to be creative, and therefore my Twenty One Summers, was limited and left me outside of that group.

My career has been steeped in the arts, as a photographer, educator, author, exhibiting artist, curator, and gallerist; yet as I sat in my apartment that day after graduation I had never been considered an artist. Feeling like you do not fit the mold of a certain lifestyle or profession can easily keep you from trying it. I certainly wasn't what an artist was "supposed to be," but luckily my career has revolved around the arts.

Many of our convictions, and expectations regarding how the world will treat us, are based on how our families lived and interacted with us. The lifestyle and rules from your home become part of you. When looking for your Blind Spots ask yourself if your parents were conservative or liberal. Did they take risks, or live life more safely? Was travel part of your childhood? Did they try new things or dream of a different life and share those dreams with you? Were there deeply held religious beliefs? Did they value hard work and hold you accountable? Did you feel safe and supported? Was your opinion appreciated and respected?

Were sports or other extra curricular activities promoted and supported? Did your parents attend your recitals, games, plays, or other events? Did they give you a lot of freedom, a little, or none at all? Often without our knowing it each of the aforementioned questions, and many others, form the ways that we interact with the world and deeply influence how we approach our lives.

Whether we view the way we were raised positively or negatively the things that we learned growing up can become Blind Spots impacting the way we make decisions, our value judgments, and how we view ourselves and the world around us. If you were listened to at home and your opinion was respected, then you will expect others to do the same. Maybe you were always busy growing up, getting outside and/or trying new things might have been encouraged, or perhaps you and your family spent more time at home. If your family spent a lot of time at home and you find yourself doing the same, take a moment and ask yourself if you are doing so because it is a habit that you formed growing up or if it is a personal choice that you are making now. These habits, good and bad, that we learn growing up become part of our identity, part of our *Who Am I, Who Am I Supposed To Be*, and *Who Can I Be*, and in doing so become Blind Spots that keep us from living our best lives.

Our spouses, partners, and children may have the same effect on the choices we make. The person that you are in a relationship with has expectations for you and the relationship. Your children will have expectations of you as a parent as well. This is in addition to their bringing opinions, ideas, and ways of acting into your home from friends, school, and other communities they are a part of.

With all of the influences at home it can become easy to end up living someone else's goals and beliefs, their *Who Am I*, at least for a while.

Your children, spouse, partner, and other family may come first, but even if you agree with the beliefs that everyone brings into your home, over time you will find yourself looking for "you" and the things that make you happy in life. I have a number of friends who would say that it is family that makes them the happiest and it makes complete sense for them to say so. But children grow up and leave the house, jobs change, spouses start new hobbies or retire and the space that family took up in your life will shift. Along with that shift come new questions about life, about what you want to make up your Twenty One Summers.

My friend Monica spent years talking about starting a new career. We met when she was an aspiring actress in Los Angeles working as a waitress and getting bit parts in various projects. She later moved to a small town in South Carolina with her new husband and started a family. Once married, Monica focused on taking care of everyone, especially their newly adopted daughter. Her *Who Am I* and *Who Should I Be* were firmly grounded in the life they had built. The family then moved to New York to support her husband's dream of getting his master's degree and becoming a film maker. They transitioned from a home in the suburbs to a small apartment in the city with grace, and she gladly took on more of the workload at home while he studied. His degree was demanding and that was followed by a challenging beginning to a new career in a new place. Excited to be in New York, Monica started going to auditions and got small parts and local commercials, but the money was inconsistent and time to audition was tight. She increasingly spoke about finding something more reliable that would help pay the bills.

Years had passed and the gap between jobs on her résumé kept growing as opportunities declined. Over time life had evolved, moving past her in a way, and she felt like the chance to make a change was passing her by. Her *Who Am I* was no longer satisfying in the same manner and *Who Can I Be* seemed an unanswerable question. Everybody at home was comfortable with who she was, but Monica needed more in her life and wanted to make a change without creating problems within the family. Frustrated, Monica wasn't sure what to do next. Then one day she gave me a call and said that she was going to apply to grad school and become a therapist. Given all of the demands in her life it was difficult to see how that was going to happen, but she had her mind set. Anxious yet driven, Monica began to look at universities across the country for an online program that would be flexible. She and others questioned her ability to get into a strong program and succeed as a student, but after sending out a number of applications, she was interviewed and accepted into the Northwestern University's Master of Arts in Counseling program. Monica was one of the oldest students in her cohort, so not only was she facing the challenge of becoming a student once again, but also learning and understanding the language, work ethic, and social perspective of a different generation. *Who Am I* was once again at play.

Getting into grad school was a big hurdle, but asking for the same time and respect at home that she had been giving her family for years was another. Though it may seem easy for some, respecting yourself and your desires enough to change household routines and ask for support can be challenging. In this case it meant changes in everyone's lifestyle and relying less on Monica during her classes and study time. Though there were bumps along the way Monica stayed strong and the family responded. She is now a licensed therapist with a full roster of clients at a private therapy practice in New York. She also has the confidence that comes from finishing her degree and achieving one of her Core Twenty One. Equally important, is the comfort of having a job that will allow her to support her family should an unexpected event occur, as well as a new *Who Am I* and *Who Can I Be*.

Sometimes the path to one of your Twenty One Summers is longer than you imagine. Finding the answer to one of her Core Twenty One proved challenging for Monica, but it also led her to a resolution that she never could have imagined just a short time ago. Monica didn't let obstacles defeat her and knew that to be happy, as well as a good partner and mother, she needed to let go of other's definitions of *Who Am I* and *Who Can I Be* and be strong enough to change herself.

Relationships, whether with a spouse, partner, or someone you are seeing, come in a range of flavors. Some are very supportive, others are not, and the rest fall in between. A once supportive partner or spouse may not want to you to go back to school, find new friends as you learn a new sport, or begin to write that book or screenplay you've always dreamed of. Children may be uncomfortable with the changes in you as you take up exercise, start cooking classes, begin teaching or volunteering, or explore a life as an artist. Finding the balance between family and your desire to effect positive change in your life can be delicate. *Who Am I, Who Am I Supposed To Be*, and *Who Can I Be* are all in play. While making room in life to take care of others, remember that your beliefs and desires are valid and deserve to be recognized too. Love, support, and embrace those who love you, and expect the same in return.

Other beliefs that form our self-identity, our *Who Am I*, come from the community around us in person and online. We define ourselves, our community, and culture in any number of ways. Clothing is one example of how we define belief systems and create a sense of belonging. As you grew up, a certain style of clothing might have been worn at your school, in your community, or at your home, and that was part of your identity. The clothing we wear is often defined by our morals, our circle of friends, and comfort with risk taking. Our clothes tell others a lot about where our boundaries lie, our lifestyle, and the community or subculture we wish to belong to. Changing the way you dress is viewed as a radical change in many communities, a signifier of acceptance or rebellion. Ask yourself if the way you dress is a personal choice or a reflection of the family and community you grew up in. Are you comfortable with your answer?

Other communal beliefs can become engrained in us as well. The way women are treated and respected is an excellent example. Was women's education and a range of career choices for girls supported in your community? Were women's rights central to the lifestyle and conversation? The way women and people of all backgrounds and lifestyles were valued in your community will affect the Blind Spots you develop and how you view and treat others. All of which will affect *Who Am I, Who Am I Supposed To Be* and *Who Can I Be*, and the dreams you pursue.

Dreams are rarely achieved without opposition and are in fact often born of those challenges. As we have learned our constraints are not always physical as friends, communities, cultures, and loved ones may ask you to stop based on their own fears, life choices, and good intentions, resulting in Blind Spots that can slow your progress. These Blind Spots create personal challenges that can cause you to question your goals and skills or take on the misgivings that come with breaking your boundaries. Yet it is in the face of these challenges that dreams prevail. This is in part what gives their achievement meaning.

The desire to dream and audacity to succeed in the face of negative messages from those around you describe the challenges and triumphs of Pasang Lhamu Sherpa Akita and Cira Crowell, two women who live on opposite sides of the world and who together have achieved more than either could have individually. Theirs is a story of women's empowerment that resonates in so many lives. One that consistently asks *Who Am I Supposed To Be, Who Can I Be*, and what that means in the context of your life and the culture in which you live.

Pasang Lhamu Sherpa Akita was born in Khumjung and raised in the small village of Lukla in the Everest Region of Nepal. During the climbing season, trekkers and mountaineers were routinely part of life in her region and views of the world's most spectacular peaks were outside of her door or just a trek away. Many of the men in her region were mountaineers and led expeditions to the summits of Everest and other mountains across the Himalayas. They were well respected and had good careers compared to many others in the region. Pasang had a love for the mountains too but grew up in a strict culture that, despite being matriarchal, limited women to home life. In Tibetan Sherpa culture, as in many places around the world, the restrictions on women and their career paths have a long tradition and in the minds of many are well intended. Yet, at the age of fifteen Pasang began to question the limitations being placed on her by her community. In doing so she initiated the move away from *Who Am I Supposed To Be*, to *Who Can I Be* and started to explore her dream of becoming a climbing instructor. Pasang refused to internalize the messages from those telling her to stop and as she grew up, she repeatedly proved herself. First by traveling to France to become Nepal's first female mountaineering instructor and then by summiting some of the world's most demanding mountains. In 2006, Pasang became the first woman to climb Nangpai Gosum II; in 2007 she summited Mount Everest; and in 2014, she was part of a three person team composed of the first Nepali women to summit K2. The latter climb was dedicated to Climate Awareness. She has also devoted time to creating opportunities for Nepali girls in the villages of her region. This was just the beginning, a beginning that started with an idea, a dream, seeing an alternative to the life she was living, moving from *Who Am I Supposed To Be* to *Who Can I Be*, and slowly, step by step, reaching one of her Core Summers, one that opened the door to many others.

Cira grew up in the polite society of the Southern United States. Her life as a young woman had been filled with horses, formal dinners, and time spent immersed in the social graces. A strong and creative student she wanted to be a photographer, but her parents did not believe that was an appropriate career for a girl. Everything in the world Cira lived in supported that assertion as the girls and women in her community often took on social and family roles. Like in Pasang's region many stayed home, raised families, and moved into the lifestyle they had grown up in. After repeatedly asking her father for a camera he finally gave in and handed Cira her grandfather's dusty camera from a shelf. The camera turned out to be a beautiful vintage Leicaflex SL2 film camera, which only strengthened her passion and resolve. Receiving a camera may seem like a small thing, but it was Cira's first step away from *Who Am I Supposed To Be* to *Who Can I Be*. Yet despite taking that step, photography as a degree path in college was still strongly discouraged. As with most things in life there were other challenges to overcome, but she had taken the first steps. Her determination to own a camera, even a dusty one off the shelf, led Cira to a new life that continues to evolve.

The changes in our lives often begin in the most unlikely places: a chance meeting, reconnecting with someone on social media, meeting a friend of a friend, a conversation over coffee. Pasang and Cira first crossed paths on Mount Rainier in the United States. Pasang was working as a guide and over the hours spent climbing the mountain they struck up a friendship that has led to over two thousand miles on mountain trails. By the time they met both women had stopped sharing their dreams with others in an unconscious effort to reduce the questions that arose when talking about their desires. Though this was a shared experience, neither knew of the silence that had overcome the other on the opposite side of the earth. Together they slowly created a space of support and understanding that helped them move beyond the negative feedback they were experiencing and into the next phase of their lives, their next set of Twenty One Summers.

Despite the vast differences in culture, location, and lifestyle, both Cira and Pasang heard messages that discouraged their personal and professional growth as others tried to define their *Who I Am* and *Who Can I Be* as young girls and women. The social and cultural definitions at work within their homes and communities were not only a product of a specific time, place, or social group; they were part of a larger system of cultural beliefs that often reduce the number of opportunities available to women and may take away their ability to decide their own future. We all face these barriers in some manner. For Cira and Pasang many of the people around them believed they were sending the right message, as it fit the norms of their community, but it also conspired to keep them from achieving the first steps toward their happiness and dreams.

Many of us hear negative messages in our lives. If you are lucky, there is a friend, partner, colleague, family member, or group there to support you when you do. Like Pasang and Cira, someone to collaborate with and create positive experiences. Even with a support system, the initial drive to make a change must come from inside of you. It will be up to you to move past negative feedback, take the first step, and build new habits by integrating small changes on a consistent basis. Your path to success may be two steps forward and one step back. That is fine, we all have setbacks. Just keep pressing forward and believing in the power of you. Find your inner strength and trust yourself. You are the best ally that anyone could have.

The way that our friends, colleagues, and acquaintances engage with us plays a large role in how we define ourselves as well. Surrounding yourself with people who value and respect you will help give you a strong positive self-identity, in the same way that someone who regularly gives you negative feedback can diminish your confidence and give you a less healthy sense of self.

Spending time in communities of like minded people or those who share a similar interest helps us find a place in the world. It can feel good to have a community where you feel you belong, and we need those anchors in life. But anchors are meant to be raised and set down again in new locations along the way. Identifying too strongly with a single company, social group, or community can create a Blind Spot, certainly all three discussed in this chapter, *Who Am I*, *Who Am I Supposed To Be* and *Who Can I Be*. If you begin to see life and its possibilities from a singular perspective you will find your options limited.

When you hold on to old definitions of *Who Am I* it may become difficult to step away from a group that provides an important part of your identity, but like the student graduating from school sometimes it is essential to let go of who you have been to move forward. Affecting change in your life and achieving your Twenty One Summers will mean that your identity and the way the world perceives you will change as you grow. It doesn't mean that you have to lose friends or walk away from your old life entirely, though you may want to do so, but it will mean allowing yourself to evolve and have friends who applaud your success.

The family, friends, and colleagues who genuinely celebrate your success are your *Pillars*. They are the people who support and believe in you. People that you can trust and confide in. They are there during good times and especially during the bad times. *Pillars* will lift you up and help you out without strings attached. They do not believe in quid pro quo, they are there for you as you should be for them. Appreciate the *Pillars* in your life, those who make you stronger and help you believe in yourself, your talents, and your ability to achieve your Twenty One Summers. True *Pillars* are rare, yet we all have them in our lives at one time or another; they may be family, friends, a loved one, someone who champions your work or has your back socially. *Pillars* come in many forms, they may be lifelong friends or someone who appears for a brief of period time in your life when you need them most. If you know someone who has been seriously ill, lost a job, or gone through a divorce, you may have been surprised at how often they have said, "The friends I expected to be there weren't, but the most unexpected person(s) stepped up." Sometimes *Pillars* come from the most unlikely places. I can personally say that I am thankful for them one and all. My parents and family were my first *Pillars*. I am also lucky enough to have a couple of lifelong friends and then there are people who out of kindness helped unexpectedly, stepping up when others did not or could not. They are all my personal heroes.

As you will see, the *Pillars* in your life will change. Friends and loved ones pass or move away. My best friend passed when he was far too young. That friendship will never be replicated. I miss him but am thankful for the amazing time spent. Other times people will drift away as they find other interests, you simply grow apart, or one of you keeps working toward their life goals while the other does not. Changes in family, health, or a personal life event may also create distance between you and someone who was a *Pillar*. Work to accept those moments in life with gratitude for what that person has given you. Let their kindness and support inspire you to do the same for others when you can.

There are many people who have helped me along the way that I wish that I could speak with one more time and others who I have been able to thank and let them know that they truly made a difference in my life. Over the past few years I have made it a point to visit friends that I may never see again if I do not take the time to do so. Why make the time to do this? Because each of these people has been a *Pillar* at one point or another, they were good friends and affected my life in a positive way. We don't choose our families or the place that we are born and raised but we can hold on to the people we meet who make our lives better and work to improve the communities that we participate in.

In his teens Yves spent much of his time photographing the city streets of Bridgeport, Connecticut, "I would take a Pentax K 1000 camera that my mom had and walk the streets of my city shooting until the entire four pack of film that I bought at Walgreens was gone. I would get super excited when they had the value pack with thirty six exposures a roll. On the weekends, I worked as a caddy for two eighteen hole rounds of golf and used what I made to process all the film and buy more. So, I would walk the streets, photographing my friends, photographing kids, you know, riding motorcycles and photographing people I knew who were homeless." People of color, like those in his community, were not represented in the books and magazines he consumed, and image makers and story tellers of color were even more rare at the time. Yves had a deep desire to tell those stories, a desire that has not gone away.

Though Yves loved photography, he didn't know that art school was an option in life. The local high school didn't provide any depth in the arts, and he felt the weight of having to be the one to take care of his immediate family financially. The decisions regarding his education needed to reflect that reality. The Blind Spots *Who Am I, Who Am I Supposed To Be*, and *Who Can I Be* were hard at work in his life. At that point, neither Yves nor his family could have envisioned the Twenty One Summers that would comprise his goals years later.

The summer before his senior year in high school Yves participated in a summer program at Wesleyan University that brought together young creatives from across the United States. Participants were selected on the basis of their work and Yves found himself in the middle of a cohort that included a diversity of talent, lifestyle, and economic standing that he had not been exposed to before. Working professionals in film, dance, and music came to instruct the aspiring artists in the program. The experience expanded Yves's sense of community and changed how his Blind Spots were functioning in his life. In Yves's case, he was introduced to a *Mentor* who became a *Teacher*. This instructor taught Yves that the world was far larger than he imagined and by the end of the summer program convinced him to apply to at least two art schools along with the other colleges he had on his list.

Teachers are people who come into your life for an extended period of time, this could be a semester or two, a year, or a lifetime. They offer knowledge, teach you lessons, provide advice and guidance, and help you through times both good and bad. You may go months or even years between seeing or speaking to a *Teacher* but they are always there for you to go to with questions, providing insight into life and helping you reach your potential. *Mentors* come into your life for a brief period of time. They may be someone you meet one time socially, a person at work or school, or an expert you are introduced to for a single conversation or short series of meetings. *Mentors* will come and go providing knowledge or insight that may resonate for the moment or stay with you throughout your life. *Teachers*, *Mentors*, and *Pillars* are the *Stars* in your life. They provide knowledge, kindness, insight, confidence, support, and so much more. They are beyond valuable.

Mentors are everywhere, you never know where they are going to come from. After the program at Wesleyan, Yves returned to school for his senior year. They didn't have a TV in their house so he would spend hours looking at photography books in the school library as he waited for his mom to get home. One day a friend told him that the librarian in the history section noticed he always carried a camera and wanted to speak with him. She had grown up with the extraordinary photographer Gordon Parks. Gordon was perhaps the most successful black photographer of the era, working for Life and Vogue magazines, among others. The librarian said that though Gordon was older and not feeling well, Yves should visit him. With that she gave Yves three of his books to study and booked a meeting for him with Mr. Parks. The librarian turned out to be an invaluable *Mentor,* she told him how to act and prepared him as best she could for their meeting. Who would have imagined the librarian at Yves's high school in Bridgeport, Connecticut, would know the most influential black photographer at the time and make an introduction that would change Yves's life and perspective?

Over the coming months Yves met Gordon Parks multiple times at his apartment in New York. They talked about photography as Gordon reviewed submissions for a grant that his foundation was offering to young image makers. All the while explaining to Yves why some photographs were good while others were not. He encouraged Yves to keep taking pictures and provided support when Yves was questioning the decisions he was making or feeling inferior to others at school. Gordon told him to take the steps necessary to find solutions as opposed to getting lost in the challenges. The knowledge gained during those conversations and friendship that emerged has filled Yves with a lifetime of memories and the desire to give back to others. Gordon Parks was an image maker and a *Teacher* right up until the end of his life and many are better for it. As you will see later in the book Yves certainly is.

When the time came to apply for college Yves sent applications to Yale, The School of Visual Arts, Parsons School of Design, Pratt, and USC. He received acceptance letters from all of them, except USC, and narrowed his choices to Parsons and Pratt. Unable to afford train fare from Bridgeport to New York he and his mother borrowed money from his grandmother to take a train ride into New York City, visiting both schools on the same day as they could not afford a second ride in. In the end they decided on Parsons, beginning the next step down the pathway toward his ever evolving Twenty One. Up to that point Yves's beliefs had been defined by life in Bridgeport and the community in which he lived. His understanding of *Who Am I* was slowly beginning to shift and *Who Am I Supposed To Be* and *Who Can I Be* were about to undergo a series of changes that continue to this day.

Changes will occur over the course of your life, whether invited or not. Like Yves, as you begin to fulfill your Twenty One Summers, your self-identity will become stronger and more actualized. You will have a deeper sense of who you are, and the satisfaction that can only come with achieving your dreams and goals big and small.

Katya wanted to learn tennis for years but always had a reason not to try. She told herself that she was too short and not athletic enough or did not have the right shoes, but the real reason she did not play was that she thought the sport was only for people from a different social class. This was a dialog that regularly happened in her family while growing up, certain things in life were for "other people." She believed this to the extent that it became a fact, or Blind Spot, never to be questioned. There were plenty of sports and other things that she could do, but it felt like you needed to be born into a certain social category to consider some sports, jobs, or lifestyles. Those beliefs seemed valid at the time, but they were now keeping her from reaching a very achievable goal. Katya didn't want to become a professional or even proficient tennis player, she just wanted to learn how to play. Once she figured out that the only thing holding her back were the Blind Spots *Who Am I* and *Who Can I Be*, it allowed her to take on the belief systems that she grew up with and to overcome them. That opened the door to contacting a tennis instructor and taking a class, finally achieving one of her Core Twenty One.

In this instance, *Who Am I* was a Blind Spot defined by a familial history that Katya knew wasn't correct but was still hard at work in her life on many levels. Even the smallest decisions can seem large when you are taking on a lifelong belief that has shaped the perception you have of yourself. *Who Am I* and *Who Can I Be* were telling her that she did not have the right body type and was not born into the right social class to do something that she wanted to do. For the longest time that made it impossible for her to visualize herself on the court with other players.

After Katya took her first tennis lessons she began to look at other areas in her life where her Blind Spots were holding her back. As she did, Katya slowly realized that she had more control over her life than she had imagined. She had been giving too much power to a perception of herself that she was completely in control of. It had been easy to live with the personal boundaries her Blind Spots created, but working through those barriers has opened up the world to her. One small action was the beginning of a substantial change. Katya is much happier now and experiencing a far richer life.

Learning tennis may seem like a small thing to you, and you may even be asking yourself how someone could be intimidated by the idea, but for Katya it was a very real challenge. The kind of challenge that we all have in our lives. Every one of us has had tasks that seemed monumental, but once when we took them on we realized how attainable they really were. This is often the case when it comes to taking the first step toward one of your Twenty One Summers and a more fulfilling life.

We can always come up with reasons not to do something, that is easy, but if you are trying to create a better life then excuses are useless. At the beginning of the semester I would often tell students that excuses are boring, and they are. Nobody wanted to spend the first fifteen minutes of class listening to others explain why something didn't happen, it was a waste of time. As a person I am sympathetic to what is happening in my student's lives, but everyone has challenges; relationships end, there are days that we don't feel our best, research for a project may be difficult, or perhaps a collaborator didn't do their share. The excuses for not finishing something are endless. Hopefully one of the things you learn in school, and in life, is how to problem solve and deliver high quality work, even when life is demanding.

Every time you succeed, especially in the face of adversity, it makes you stronger. It expands your capabilities and increases your capacity. There is always an excuse for not achieving something you want in life. Don't let those excuses undermine your ability to succeed.

Excuses and rationalizations often turn into procrastination, chipping away at your time as it slowly takes away your dreams. Each day, month, or year that you wait to take that first step makes achieving your goals harder. This is another reason to clearly define your Twenty One Summers and begin moving toward them. Once goals are clarified and excuses are set aside you can start taking small steps forward. Like Monica, Pasang, Cira, and Yves, the path forward may not always be a straight one, but if you persevere and value the time you have been given, you will prevail. At the end of our lives we do not regret time well spent, but the things we have not tried or achieved.

A few months ago I went to the Metropolitan Museum of Art and discovered a series of photographs from New

York in the early 1900s. Each scene was rich with history, but I found myself looking at the people more than the setting. These were pictures of people living everyday life, working class men and women selling goods on the street or from proprietor owned shops, and doing the manual labor necessary to build an early version of the city we know today. Looking into their eyes I wondered about the struggles they faced, whether they chose their jobs and lifestyle or took the work that was available to earn a living. I imagined the drive it must have taken to move to New York and start a new life for themselves or their families and wondered if they had achieved their hopes and dreams in some way. It was a reminder of the balance between the choices we make in life, the challenges and opportunities we are given, and how brief life really is. Everyone in each of those photographs has long since passed. Whatever their aspirations, they took them with them when they died.

When future generations see photographs of you and look into your eyes will they see someone who had hope, dreams? Someone who was working toward the best life that they can live? Will they imagine a person who made choices and took on the things necessary to make their short time here fulfilling? Will they see someone who was inspired and inspired those around them? Someone who was making the most of every moment, working toward their Twenty One Summers? What they will see is up to you: choice is yours.

We can never know what opportunities exist on the other side of change, but good things often arise in the most unlikely moments. This idea has been at work for my entire life. Remember the job at the movie theater? I could never have imagined working there growing up, yet I had to have a job if I wanted to stay in Los Angeles and pursue my dream of working in the film industry. Leaving Los Angeles would have meant letting those opportunities slip away. It was my first big step away from home and the *Who Am I* of the first part of my life, so I kept taking tickets and serving popcorn as I learned more about the city and the movie business. Unbeknownst to me the theater hosted movie premieres. While it was beyond exciting for a boy from a small town to see and meet famous actors, directors, and producers, it was a much smaller interaction that changed my career path and my life.

One day, a friend of the theater manager came in; he was casting director for background actors and small parts in TV, movies, and music videos. We got to know each other a bit and one day he said, "Why are you working at the theater? We need to get you out of here!" and he got me a job as an assistant casting director at the company he worked at. I was, and still am, thankful for the opportunity, but I didn't stay in film long as I quickly learned the industry was not what I imagined. Casting did give me access to an endless number of people to photograph as most everyone wanted to meet a casting director, even an assistant casting director, and I began to build my portfolio as a photographer. My *Who Am I* and *Who Can I Be* had just changed. Without knowing it, I was taking the first step toward starting my career as a photographer.

Derrick didn't stay at the company where they kicked him awake in the morning. He and his new girlfriend, now wife, had saved one thousand dollars. It was 1992, flights were cheap, and they had enough money to go backpacking in Mexico so they headed to Mexico City. After crisscrossing the country in buses for three months he got tired of sitting on the beach and knew that it was time to get back to work. They returned to the UK and decided to go to Dublin instead of London as his girlfriend Debbie wanted to do something different. After they arrived, a small tech employment agency suggested he apply for a job at a company called Microsoft. They had a small office in Dublin and the agency thought it might be a good fit. There wasn't any internet in 1992 and Windows wasn't a very widely used program, so Derrick went to the local library to find a few articles about Microsoft in fledgling tech magazines. During his job interview they asked him how well he knew Microsoft Windows and he started to talk about UNIX Windows, a program created by another company. Not a stellar start to his career, but his knowledge of programming was deep and they brought him on board.

Little did Derrick's parents know that when they bought him a Big Trek programmable electric vehicle and a sixty dollar ZX81 home computer with 1KB of memory, that it was the beginning of a way of life for their son. Taking the job at Microsoft, a rather unknown company at the time, was the next step into an entirely new industry. One that with time, hard work, focus, a few risks, and a willingness to see technology and the world in a different way than his peers, has brought about changes that have affected the way we all live.

Life's changes come in a range of experiences. Many like graduation or retirement are expected and we can plan for them, but others take us by surprise. Imagine the unexpected challenges faced by a successful football player or dancer transitioning into a new life after an injury ends their career, or someone in the military coming home after a difficult deployment. Getting divorced, losing a job, or the early loss of a loved one are unexpected events that will affect many of our lives. After a life changing event your self-identity and place in the world are altered and our first three Blind Spots *Who Am I*, *Who Am I Supposed To Be*, and *Who Can I Be* immediately come into play as our Twenty One Summers shift and we have to take the first steps down a new path in life.

Questions regarding your Twenty One Summers also happen during times of positive change. A new love or relationship may cause you to reconsider your goals, the way you may spend your time, and the trajectory of your life. Having children and starting a family will do the same. Things that seemed important before may not have the same relevance. A new and unexpected job can change your outlook personally and financially; it may also mean having to decide whether to relocate. Positive changes in life change don't need to be large, it could be a change in diet that helps you lose twenty one pounds, or perhaps taking an art class and discovering that you love drawing. When these events occur, check your Blind Spots to be sure they aren't holding you back and review your Twenty One to see if you want or need to make any changes. Embracing goodness when it happens can be surprisingly hard to do sometimes. Open your life to happiness and the opportunities that the world provides, they are a gift.

One of the greatest changes in my *Who Am I* and *Who Can I Be* came over the last few months of 2019. I had recently left New York and as part of that transition put together a series of international projects with Chinese partners. Working in New York and internationally had become important parts of my identity as they were central to my life, personal growth, and career. I missed New York but it wasn't until after the pandemic wiped out all of my travel, public speaking, and new global projects, that I understood the real challenge that was facing me. A large portion of my Twenty One were suddenly gone. I had to rebuild and redefine my life. *Who Am I, Who Am I Supposed To Be*, and *Who Can I Be* loomed large. I needed to resolve all three Blind Spots if I was going to move forward.

There were other complications as well. In late November of that year I had a double pulmonary embolism on a flight to the United States from China. The main arteries to both of my lungs were blocked by blood clots severely restricting the blood supply and my lungs' ability to function. I had gotten up to use the restroom and woke up some time later sitting fully dressed with my head in my hands. There wasn't any memory of sitting down or how long I had been in there, but when I opened the restroom door the gentleman outside looked quite upset, so it must have been a while. I began to walk back to my seat but about three rows down I passed out in the aisle. The next thing I knew I was watching three men lift me up. It was as if I was sitting in one of the rows looking at myself, head down, body limp. When one of the men asked a woman if they could use her seat I was suddenly back in my body watching the woman exit as they placed me into the second row. A doctor on board had the flight attendants give me oxygen, which made all the difference. The attendant suggested I lay down but it was difficult to breathe and I didn't want to let go of the back of the seat in front of me. It was a good thing, as I later learned when you have an embolism your heart pumps harder as it tries get blood into your lungs and in doing so it enlarges. If I had laid down I would have most likely had a heart attack.

The doctors at the hospital also told me that you have a thirty three percent chance of not waking up when you pass out from an embolism, and I had passed out twice.

At one point, a flight attendant leaned over the seat in front of me to talk with the doctor about what might have happened. They quickly became faint and blurry, and seemed as if they were far away. Then a bright voice above the left side of my head said, "So, you don't have a family, you're not in a relationship, you don't have a full-time job. Do you want to stay?" My voice, just above my head, said, "I wonder what I'm going to say?" A reply came from another bright sounding voice on my lower right, "Yes, I want to stay! I love my friends and my family. I like what I do! I like my life." To which the voice on the left replied, "OK." All of a sudden, I was moving forward through a blurry tunnel and in an instant the doctor was next to me again with the flight attendant still there chatting with him. Everything was crystal clear and I thought to myself, "Well, I've made my decision, now it is up to them and my body." There was never any fear or concern, just a deep sense of peace throughout the experience. It was a moment of deep learning. I understood how some people wait until everyone arrives before passing while others wait until everyone leaves the room. Sometimes, we have a choice.

Despite everything that had happened I believed that it would all be fine. The paramedics met the plane and the emergency room rallied. During the first few hours of getting tests and moving in and out of the emergency room I overheard a conversation between two interns as one wondered aloud if I would make it. That brought a moment of questioning that I had to put aside so that I could focus on staying present, listening, and learning how to heal.

There were times when I felt alone while in the ICU. I wondered if the tubes would be removed, the machines would ever go away, and I would be myself again, but the doctors did a great job from my arrival until leaving. Luckily it all worked out and after four and a half days in intensive care and a day in a regular room, I was released.

As I healed the event became empowering, helping me realize that I had more choices in life than imagined. I was heartened by survival and inspired to appreciate life and value each day, but it did not change the professional reality that I faced. In fact, it made me even more aware of the need to let go of presumptions and take risks in my career. Trying things that I had previously avoided.

I don't tell this story out of a sense of drama or for sympathy. It is here for four reasons: time, choice, effort, and gratitude. Time, because our time here is limited. I have always appreciated life and all that it brings, but perhaps a bit more now as every additional moment seems a gift, one to be used to its greatest advantage. Though this experience wasn't the genesis of Twenty One Summers, I had been teaching and living Twenty One Summers for years, it certainly gave me a new perspective regarding the need to do more now instead of waiting for later. Choice, because the choice to stay and continue my work was one of the most powerful realizations from the experience. It is a decision that inspires and empowers me daily. We make choices like that throughout our lives, whether it is to love or support someone, to treat ourselves and others better, work toward living our dreams, devote ourselves to the effort and discipline it takes to reach goals large and small, or to enjoy the beauty of the good people around us and the magic of the day. That doesn't mean everything is perfect, it isn't, but how we choose to engage with everyone and everything in our lives makes all the difference. You can complain and view everything as an irritating negative or do your best to work to make things better. It is your choice. At this point I spend far less time around people and things that diminish life and more time with those that make it better, and that has led to some interesting changes. It was hard to let go of some friendships, acquaintances, bad habits, and ways of doing things, but life is increasingly better for it. Effort, because of the effort it took to rebuild my health and career, neither of which seemed guaranteed at the time. Also, the effort of those around me who continue to inspire by building extraordinary lives, taking on new challenges and growing daily, being good people, and helping others along the way. Whether you like it or not, hard work is a key to attaining your goals and changing your life. There is no way around it, and that is absolutely OK. Gratitude, because now it permeates most everything that I do on some level. I have always been thankful for many things in life and still am, but lately I experience greater gratitude for an ever evolving Twenty One that challenges me daily. Life indeed continues to surprise.

It took a while to rebuild my *Who Am I* and *Who Can I Be*. I wasn't sure if I would fully recover physically or if my career would ever be the same. Everything had to be redefined. The process was challenging but at this point I have achieved more physically than I ever thought possible, including climbing and trekking in the Himalayan Mountains of Nepal and exercising almost daily. I unexpectedly cried when my girlfriend and I reached the top of Gokyo Ri (17,575 feet) during our first trip to Nepal in 2023. I finally knew that I was healing and it was possible to overcome the damage done by the embolism. The physical and mental release was empowering, motivating me to work even harder. This was a new step in understanding *Who Can I Be* and an important point in its continued change. My career had evolved as well, I was now consulting, writing more, public speaking, giving workshops, sitting on not for profit boards, and traveling to teach classes and individuals one on one. The change was welcome and has led to new and unexpected experiences, as a new set of Twenty One Summers can do.

When life changing events happen it is up to you to set the tone for how others will view you. The power to do so is within your grasp. If you take on change in a positive self determined manner others and life will react to you in the same way. Sure, it will be a lot of work in the beginning. Many will hold on to old definitions of you or spend their time mourning your past as opposed to helping you build your future. But if you decide to find a new vision for yourself, to be proactive and try new things, others will begin to see you in new and empowered ways. You will find that you begin to attract people who believe in you and celebrate the positive changes in your life. Most important, you will be redefining your life and not letting your Blind Spots do it for you.

There have been a number of times in my life when loss and change were the driving factors. Many of those times were challenging, but thankfully the desire to be happy and successful won in the end. Sometimes that meant the loss of past histories, communities, and people I believed were friends, but the real friends always stayed, and many provided priceless support and acceptance. New friends and colleagues entered my life as well and provided the impetus to live life in new and unexpected ways. The clearly defined goals and desires of your Twenty One Summers will give you stability during challenging times and help provide a pathway forward. Don't hold too tightly on to old definitions. Let your life be filled with new possibilities. That is a beautiful thing about working on your Twenty One: you never know where they are going to take you. It is impossible to know all of the possibilities in your life before you start exploring.

Chapter Three
Make Me Comfortable

Growing up I used to tease my Mom, saying that if I had listened to her I would have ended up playing the violin and knitting as opposed to riding a motorcycle and heading out on adventures. Knitting and the violin are worthy pastimes and wonderful careers of course, and her concern came from her love and desire to keep me safe, as parents do. Though she and my father supported and celebrated my adventures, failures, and successes, my mother would have been more comfortable if I had listened and not taken some of the risks that I have. If I had done so my life would have been very, very different. Wonderful, but not the beautiful, challenging, unexpected ride that it has been.

As mentioned in the last chapter, people often ask you to change your goals, alter the way you live, follow their beliefs, or live their lifestyle and traditions, out of good intentions. They may be concerned for your safety, your future, or truly believe they know the best path to your happiness and success. This advice, however well intended, is a Blind Spot. You see, whether well intended or not people often offer comments or advice because what you are doing makes them uncomfortable. That discomfort may come from fear or personal experiences that do not directly apply to your life, or because you are taking a path that diverges from what has worked for them or from local tradition. To be clear, we aren't saying that you should disregard all of the advice you receive from your parents, family, or friends. It is important to listen to feedback from those around you, but equally important not to let it define you. Whether at work, home, with friends, or in your community, others love to keep you within their comfort zone; they want you to *Make Me Comfortable*, a Blind Spot that affects us all. Living within someone else's comfort zone may seem easy, but you can't reach your Twenty One Summers living someone else's life.

Not only do others want us to *Make Them Comfortable* to the point that we hold ourselves back, we do the same thing to ourselves. When you become overly comfortable with your knowledge, skills, community, career, or lifestyle, it can become increasingly difficult to make a positive change in your life. You may begin to fear change, embrace inaction, or worry about feeling uncomfortable as your life evolves. Somehow becoming a stronger and more positive person can seem more difficult than living unhappily or letting bad habits ruin your life. One of the reasons for this is *Make Me Comfortable*.

Whether at work or home, ignoring your Twenty One Summers and avoiding positive change to please others is not a sustainable option. Frustration will mount and resentment may build. It is almost impossible to completely satisfy someone else, or everyone else, without losing yourself in the process.

We all know the phrase "peer pressure" and often associate it with being a child, but it functions in various forms throughout our lives. There are times when peer pressure can become so common and pervasive that we acquiesce to the beliefs and desires of others without even thinking about it; this too is a Blind Spot.

Though we like to think of ourselves as individuals, we often find ourselves consciously or unconsciously conforming to group or community standards. There are a number of reasons we do so, many of which are positive in nature while others are unhealthy. We might conform in order to make a group, company, or organization function more smoothly. Some organizations like the military demand conformity in terms of logistics, hierarchy, and organization. It is essential to their operational success and lives literally depend on it. Conforming to the rules and cultural norms in an operating room as a doctor, nurse, or intern will save lives as well. Every business needs to be able to depend on a certain level of conformity in terms of professionalism, organization, continuity, systems, client engagement, public messaging, and teamwork to be successful. Small businesses, not-for-profits, and corporate cultures ask for varying levels of conformity in terms of the style of doing business in the workplace, time demands, effort, and adherence to the mission of the organization. Our lives and society in general run more smoothly when we treat each other and the places we live and work with respect.

When cultures are positive in nature, your participation in them will benefit both you and the organization. In toxic work cultures, the undermining of others, spread of gossip, and the adherence to toxic and destructive ways of engaging with colleagues and clients are unhealthy ways of conforming. Doing so can be destructive to yourself and the organization. The same applies to social groups and personal relationships. When you find yourself in one of these situations it is time for a change. Change that is in your best interest, a shift that moves you toward your Twenty One and a more satisfying way of living.

You may think that toxic environments are rare, but there are acquaintances, friends, family members, social communities, and businesses that will work to undermine your confidence and keep you from succeeding. In these situations the pressure to conform may come through compliments, bullying, threats, being given rewards or having them withheld, alienation from a social group or committees and events within your organization, being given less desirable projects, or a number of other processes that may manipulate or coerce you into conforming to toxic methods of engagement and an unhealthy environment. Some people will want you to do less at work or in your personal life as it makes them feel more comfortable about their place in things, beliefs, power, or success. Their goal can be twofold, as it may help ensure their happiness and success at the cost of your own.

There are people who thrive by creating toxicity and chaos, engaging with the world in a manner that diminishes others' ability to realize their true potential. Let that knowledge motivate you to take the first steps away from toxic individuals, organizations, and negative forms of conformity. That may mean creating distance between you and those in your life who do not support you or make your life better while spending more time with your *Stars* (*Pillars, Teachers, Mentors*), and supportive family, colleagues, and friends. Your circle of friends and acquaintances may become smaller, but it will be stronger, more positive, and more supportive. When you find yourself in a toxic situation at work consider changing roles within your organization, moving to a new company, or changing fields to something better suited to you, your skills, and your personality.

As a tech executive in his twenties Derrick was highly competitive, driven by a desire to succeed, competing more with others than himself. He was relentless, taking on as much as he could while leaving others on his team behind when they could not keep up. In yearly reviews he would hear that he should slow down because his pace and effort were making some of his colleagues uncomfortable. Derrick's attitude changed after receiving feedback from one of his managers who turned out to be a *Mentor*. As Derrick described, "I didn't really consider how my performance might impact my colleagues. However, as I entered my thirties, I began to realize that my competitive approach was not sustainable in the long term. I found relationships with my colleagues were suffering and it was tiring to continuously compete with myself and others. I was spending a lot of time thinking about why my skills were not as good as colleagues in adjacent fields." Everyone who is successful is competitive in some manner, but taking it to an extreme and wanting to win all of the best projects and awards can hold you back as opposed to helping you get ahead.

Yet there is a twist to the story. Derrick did learn to slow down, but while his colleagues may have become more comfortable, he was not. He was not challenging himself and working below his capacity was making him very unhappy. Ultimately, slowing down was detrimental to his success. Working at the same pace as everyone else did not allow him to distinguish himself, nor was he growing creatively and intellectually. So he found a combination that made sense for him by managing creative teams and projects in a more collaborative context. He was able to bring together teams of people who were similarly driven and create cultures in which the entire team was challenged professionally and intellectually. Some people loved being part of a fast-paced groundbreaking team, while others opted to work in environments that were less demanding. Both outcomes were positive, as it allowed everyone involved to find their place at the company.

Getting away from people who are uncomfortable with you working toward your Twenty One is not always as easy as changing departments at work. There are times when it may feel almost impossible to avoid toxic environments. That is when you need to prioritize yourself, taking the first steps away from toxic individuals and toward realizing your potential. Move away from those who would hold you back and into a more positive and fulfilling life.

As a society we celebrate the idea of following your dreams and achieving independence and success outside of the local norms, yet some individuals and communities view a person who does so as a bad influence as opposed to someone to be emulated or respected. They often seek to drive those people away instead of celebrating their success or embracing a new perspective and learning from it. Why would anyone be uncomfortable with a person who had similar beginnings but made different yet positive choices in life? Because we get caught up in fear and comparisons.

At some point in our lives we all compare ourselves to others, feeling as if someone else's success magnifies our perceived failure or lack of achievement. Comparison drives some people to minimize and undermine those moving ahead or to alienate them altogether, believing it is better to negate others, impede their growth, or belittle their achievements, than it is to embrace positive change and grow themselves. They incorrectly presume life will be easier if everyone around them is less motivated and thinks, acts, and lives like they do. This is all done in an effort to *Make Themselves Comfortable*.

One way to remove comparisons from your life is to compete against yourself and not others. It is easy to feel as if the people around you or on social media are achieving more than you are. Don't fall into that trap; gauge the new you against the old you. You can never truly win when competing against someone else. You may find success in life, but there will always be someone in the world who is smarter, richer, more talented, more successful, or in better shape than you, and that is absolutely fine. Even if you are lucky enough to reach the pinnacle of your sport or profession, setting records along the way, life changes and careers end. You have to be ready to adapt your Twenty One, often unexpectedly.

After my first job out of college I felt like some friends had such a big head start in terms of their lives and careers that I would never catch up. Casting background and spending time on movie and TV sets had been a great learning experience, but it wasn't a career nor was it going to give me what I wanted out of life. So five years after graduating from the University of Wisconsin I found myself at The Art Center College of Design in Pasadena learning how to become a better photographer. The knowledge, network, and inspiration that I received there were priceless, but school set me back another four years plus the cost of tuition, two things that seemed insurmountable.

I did finally catch up with my friends, but the years in between were a challenge. *Who Can I Be* was hard at work in my life. I did not feel jealousy, nor did I have a problem with anyone else's success. I was happy for them, as I was competing against myself. This was about my life, lifestyle, health, peace, and happiness, that was not something to take lightly.

We manifest *Make Me Comfortable* in many ways. A few years ago, I was in Michigan's Upper Peninsula visiting friends. It was a cold snowy night in a beautifully wooded rural area covered with fresh white snow and few people on the road. I stopped at a small corner tavern to grab a bite to eat. The only person there was the bartender, and as I sat at the end of the bar there were rows of empty seats to my left and right. While I waited for my food, three men walked in wearing Cat snowmobile suits, representing their Caterpillar snowmobiles. They had ridden their snowmobiles to the bar together and spent their time telling stories and laughing as they enjoyed a beer. About thirty minutes later, another snowmobiler showed up and to my surprise he sat alone on the other side of the bar. The first group ignored him for a while and then one man noticed he was wearing a Polaris snowmobile suit and had ridden up on a Polaris snowmobile. The first three men began to give him a hard time about his snowmobile and then about pretty much everything else they could think of. It became so uncomfortable that the man in the Polaris suit quietly left the bar not finishing his beer or meal.

These four men could not have had more in common with one another. They were all the same race, in their mid to late forties, and given the area and their conversation they were all working class and making a good enough living to own snowmobiles. They were dressed similarly, all liked snowmobiling, corner bars, and a beer with their dinner. The first group never called the other man by name, so I assumed they did not know him. The only discernible difference between them that night was the brand of snowmobiles they rode and the name on their snowsuits. Instead of finding comradery in that shared moment on a cold winter evening those men looked for one difference and turned it into a reason to send someone back out into the night. It *Made Them Comfortable* to do so as they found community in the alienation of another. This is not a trait unique to any one group. Individuals and communities often look for a way to create identity, whether that is spending time together, finding commonality in clothes, beliefs, actions, habits, and ways of living and playing, or using the same to exclude others.

It does not take a grand gesture to make others uncomfortable, small things like a snowmobile suit can do it as well. You never know how someone will react to the things you do. If life so far is any lesson, people will often surprise you with their response to your differences, personal growth, or the things you love. Stay strong when others have negative reactions to good things happening to you, or place roadblocks in your path. Don't trade your happiness to make someone else comfortable. If someone truly loves or supports you they won't try to limit your dreams with their actions or words, they will want to see you blossom.

I've always wondered why a negative or demeaning attitude seems to pervade some people. So many seem to have more reasons not to change than they do to make life better. Do you know people who always have a negative comment or rebuttal that accompanies every positive thing you say or do? Are complaints and things that go wrong consistently part of their everyday conversation? People don't always hold you back by commenting directly about what you are doing; they may also wear you down with negative commentary. For some this commentary is conscious, for others it is habit. Either way, it is detrimental to you and your ability to progress. Not recognizing when this is happening in your life is a Blind Spot. That too will keep you from your true potential.

Certainly not all communities are negative, nor do they ask you to give up your individuality to belong. When you find a supportive community, one that provides useful information and helps you feel stronger as you grow, embrace it. Communities like these are a good thing as they can offer support while you move through changes in your life. Always be aware of the point when support becomes expectation and you are not able to be yourself anymore. If you find your thoughts, happiness, lifestyle, and opinions are silenced or diminished, it is time to take the first step toward moving on.

When walking to class at the University of Wisconsin Madison, I used to pass a cart where a gentleman in his seventies was selling posters that he had made himself. On one he had drawn three pigs, one of which was happily sitting in the mud. Underneath them was the phrase, "Never get in the mud with a pig. Remember, the pig likes it there." I think of that phrase often when running into toxic or destructive people in life. You can choose to try to take them on at their own game, but if you do, remember that for whatever reason they live that game twenty four hours a day, seven days a week, and you do not.

Work toward positive change in your life and over the long run you will grow past those who would prefer to hold you back or make you feel as if you will never get ahead. Of course, doing so means hard work, focus, valuing your time, and a dedication to making changes in your life. If you stay focused on yourself, one day you will realize that you have left those toxic people and situations far behind and grown in ways they did not want you to. You will be achieving your Twenty One Summers and enjoying the happiness, understanding, knowledge and lifestyle that come along with them.

Be aware that the Blind Spot *Make Me Comfortable* will happen throughout your life. You may be told what constitutes a good career, where you should be living, what lifestyle you should live, the hobbies and activities that make you valid, and what your aspirations should be. This is particularly evident after graduation, though it happens mid-life and upon retirement as well.

After teaching at a university and watching so many people head out into their lives you realize how formative the first few years after graduation can be. In addition to working through the Blind Spot *Who Can I Be*, mistakes are made, successes are often hard won, and there may be struggles as students move into the real world and begin to understand what they really want to do in life. That is not only normal, but healthy, as new coping mechanisms are developed and the first steps are taken along the pathway to a different life. This process can be hard to watch, but oftentimes the fear we feel is our own. When this happens, do not let your own need to feel comfortable prevent someone you love from taking on challenges and living a rich and fulfilling life.

A few of years ago an acquaintance's daughter moved to New York to explore her dream of working in the theater. That first year was rough. Finding jobs in the theater, building a network, and sustaining a comfortable lifestyle were not easily achieved and after twelve months she decided to move back home. It was a difficult choice but one that seemed prudent. Her mother, a good parent, was supportive of her return and was happy when her daughter found a local job. It wasn't in theater, but it was comfortable and had a future, if a limited one. It would be misleading if I didn't say that her mother was happy to have her daughter living nearby. Many parents would feel this way.

I have met a number of parents who have felt relieved when their son or daughter's investigation of another city is over and they are now safely back home. What catches my attention is how happy some are that their child's time away exploring life and its possibilities has ended. I haven't always found their children as excited about the job or lifestyle they find themselves in. There is often a loss of wonder and a sense of resignation. It is in these instances that I realize some parents' desire to have their children live nearby comes from the Blind Spot *Make Me Comfortable*. Their fears, worries, lack of experience, or longing to have a companion to fill a void in life, perhaps after a divorce or becoming an empty nester, are central to urging their children to return. To be clear, we are not talking about instances where there are larger social or personal issues at play or when someone is being self-destructive. Moments like those require far more attention and the move back to a safer place is a good one. We are however talking about times when the parent's desire supersedes healthy exploration and personal growth.

It is heartening to hear parents talk about helping their child get back on their feet and examine the lessons learned from their experience before heading back out into the world to build their own lives and fulfill their Twenty One. It is hard to see your child struggle or fail, but they will learn, like all of us do. We succeed, fail, learn from these experiences, and then apply that knowledge as we move on. That is how we learn to navigate the world.

Fine art photographer Elinor Carucci had a slightly different experience. As a young image maker in Israel Elinor wanted to publish a book of her work but her photographs were not well received by local teachers and acquaintances. People in her hometown told her that her photographs were "boring" or that she was "going nowhere." It can be hard not to internalize comments like these as they bring up the Blind Spots *Who Am I, Who Am I Supposed To Be*, and *Who Can I Be*. Each time she heard this feedback, it caused her to question herself and she wondered if her dream of being a photographer and seeing her work in print would ever happen. Then one day some visitors from America reviewed her photographs and responded far more positively.

The positive feedback she received helped Elinor move out of her comfort zone and take a chance that was supported by her family. Her mother said, "Why don't you try going to New York?" So with her parents' blessing she traveled to the States. It was a big risk, Elinor did not know a lot of people in New York, nor did she understand the way that business was done in the worlds of art and publishing in America. Yet she persevered and learned as she moved toward her dream. Though the path has been a long and winding one, Elinor's determination and love for creating ultimately prevailed. In 2019 Elinor published her fourth monograph titled *Midlife*, perhaps the best received of her four books to date.

It is fair to say that much of Elinor's success would not have occurred without her parents' support. *Make Me Comfortable* was not at work in Elinor's relationship with her family. Their belief in her talent and willingness to participate in her photographs was an important part of Elinor's Core Twenty One.

Creatively, Elinor pushed against the borders of her comfort zone photographing her parents and her family's personal life with honesty and integrity. In doing so, Elinor has taken on *Who Can I Be* and *Make Me Comfortable* regularly throughout her career.

Publishing four monographs, representation by a leading New York gallery, numerous awards, photographs in museum collections, and regular editorial assignments certainly equates success, but that does not mean that things have come easy for Elinor or that the path has been always comfortable. As she described, "I have not given up, but sometimes when I'm having a bad day, I doubt my talent. I doubt my choices. I doubt the financial concerns that come with the instability and income that is not always consistent. In those moments I threaten to give up. I'm like, 'That's it!' I have those days when I say, 'I can't do it anymore!' I'm going to be, 'You know, I used to be a professional belly-dancer. I'm going to teach belly-dancing in the gym, and this is it!,' but then I don't do it, and I get up the next day or the day after and write some emails and make a list of things I want to photograph, or work on my current project and I don't give up."

We all have moments of doubt. Own those moments, live them, and then let them go. Don't take them into your next day or your projects and relationships. Instead focus on small successes like doing some research or writing an email that takes you one step closer to realizing your Twenty One. As an artist or businessperson a certain amount of risk is part of building a successful career. Failure is built into the process, it is unavoidable, but that is not necessarily a bad thing. Elinor has repeatedly overcome challenges, rejection, and failures as she has built an extraordinary career as a fine art and commercial photographer. With each photograph that she creates and each book published she learns and grows, evolving along the way.

Art, design, and technology all incorporate something called the Iterative Process in the creation of new work or products. One of the things that makes the Iterative Process so valuable is that it acknowledges failure and the need to repeat a process multiple times as a core component for reaching a successful outcome or final result.

As an educator in the arts, the Iterative Process is always part of my classroom. Students propose a project, define the steps they will take to begin the project, implement those steps, begin to create photographs or work in other media, and then present the work for feedback and critique. When a photograph does not live up to expectations it signals a student's need to develop stronger production skills, grow their creative skill set, improve their ability to articulate a concept, expand their references, or problem-solve unexpected challenges. Critique and healthy feedback help students understand where the process needs work and provides insight into how they might move forward with the next iteration of their photographs. With each iteration the pictures become stronger technically, conceptually, in terms of production, or as a body of work. The student's ability to describe their work improves as well.

These are considered Moments of Learning, times when falling short of your goal provides an opportunity to identify the areas in which you need to grow and to develop new methods of problem solving to address them. Each of us are faced with Moments of Learning throughout our lives. The challenge is to move past *Make Me Comfortable* and use these experiences to help us better understand *Who Can I Be* and the steps to get there.

Whether you are aware of it or not, we all utilize the Iterative Process as we work toward our Twenty One. For athletes, artists, bakers, musicians, writers, and so many others, the Iterative Process is central to learning new perspectives and developing new skills. Every repetition is filled with Moments of Learning. With each iteration they get a little bit better, moving closer to achieving their goals and of course their Twenty One. We understand and respect the fact that it takes time to become a better artist, chess player, writer, skier, or cook. There will be artwork thrown away, moves made that cost a queen or a king, multiple drafts of a chapter written, falls on moguls, meals burnt, and lessons learned with each repetition or iteration. Failures are simply part of the process. I wonder why we don't extend that same understanding to ourselves as we learn new things, change our careers, or work improve our personal lives? Why don't we look at our challenges or failures as Moments of Learning and apply the Iterative

Process to the skills we want to learn and ways we need to grow? If you do so, over time you will see your old self in the rear-view mirror and be surprised at how far you have come.

When speaking to young photographers I often ask them to think of their favorite photographer and the photographs by that image maker that they can see in their mind. I then ask them how many photographs they remember. The answer is generally between ten and twelve. I then point out that the twelve images they remember are a small portion of the hundreds if not thousands of photographs by the photographer that were good enough to appear in editorials, ad campaigns, or exhibitions. That does not include the hundreds of thousands of photographs that were not good enough to appear in print, online, in a gallery or museum, or in advertising. The amount of failure and Moments of Learning that it took to create the dozen photographs each student remembers is extraordinary. It is a lifetime of engaging in the Iterative Process, moving away from *Make Me Comfortable*, learning from each success or failure, and the changing expectations from clients and others along the way. If a student can only remember twelve photographs by one of the greatest artists in their field, then perhaps they need to give themselves a break and allow themselves to fail from time to time along the road to their Twenty One Summers.

The same idea applies to your favorite musician or soccer player. How many wrong notes were played or goals missed along the way to becoming one of the greats? How many hours were spent repeating scales and rehearsing songs or in practice dribbling the ball, passing, and taking shots on goal? How many bad meals were cooked on the way to becoming an Iron Chef? The people that you admire have used and lived the Iterative Process throughout their lives. You can apply it to projects big and small.

In tech, the Iterative Process is regularly used as hardware and software are developed. For instance, in 1971, Intel introduced the first programmable microprocessor. This was the first step in the development of less expensive, faster processors that would allow desktop computers and then laptops and phones to proliferate. Using the Iterative Process, Intel experimented with different materials, creating progressively smaller faster processors that allowed the company and related industries to flourish. There were certainly many failures along the way, but the engineers learned from each experiment, applying their knowledge to what at the time seemed to be an endless series of ever-improving products. Nvidia is following the same process as they develop the chips that power AI.

For most of us, AI burst onto the scene in 2022 when ChatGPT was introduced by OpenAI. Launched on the Bing search engine, people signed up on a wait list for the chance to use the application. Using ChatGPT in 2022 was different than using Google or Bing to search for information online. You knew that this was the beginning of a change in the way things were done. Debates over whether the introduction of AI was positive or negative raged, and users felt like they were on the cutting edge of technology. Now millions of people across the world are signing into ChatGPT using it in their personal lives and businesses. What most people didn't know at the time was that six hundred sixty million online users and more than a billion people on smartphones and pads were already engaging daily with a Chinese AI-powered chatbot named Xaioice.

A Microsoft team led by Derrick created this technological breakthrough using the Iterative Process. The process began with Xaioice talking to a small number of people every day. Through repetition the program learned which responses worked, which responses did not work, and most importantly how to hold a long, productive, and enjoyable conversation with each user. Over time people were asking her for advice on how to date, apply for jobs, and improve their social skills, in much the same way they would ask a human friend.

To be clear, there were many failures during Xiaoice's development process as both the program and the engineers had a lot to learn along the way. Everyone had to face *Make Me Comfortable*, as this project was a big risk for the engineers and the company. In 2014, few people were thinking about AI and even fewer believed in its potential. It took a handful of people advocating for Xiaoice to keep the project alive and take it to fruition.

You may face similar doubts in life from yourself and the people around you. As we know, people have their own Blind Spots and agendas, and they do not always include helping you get ahead. Just like Derrick and his team in the early days building Bing or developing AI. They faced people who were not comfortable with their efforts or simply did not believe in them, but today Bing is a successful search engine for Microsoft and AI has become an important part of their Azure Cloud, Office, Bing, CoPilot, and other businesses, not to mention a number of the company's new products. If Derrick and his bosses had listened to those who wanted to halt either project Microsoft would be a very different company today. The lesson for you is to keep moving forward and believe in yourself. You never know what you will achieve in the face of other's doubts and limitations.

One big difference between humans and AI is that AI can learn objectively from its mistakes. When the program understands an answer or outcome is incorrect, it tucks that information away and moves forward without attaching an emotion to the failure. Most people fear failure, they avoid it for the fear of looking foolish, being reprimanded, feeling uncomfortable, or because of what they were told about failing as a child or adult. Moments of failure can trigger all of our Blind Spots and we can become overwhelmed. The way AI learns is an example of failure as a positive, particularly if you can remove the negative emotional and social connotations from the action or word. Doing so will allow you to take risks, engage in the Iterative Process, and grow personally and professionally. This is a powerful lesson for us all.

The value of risk-taking and failing was a lesson Derrick learned from the then Microsoft CEO Steve Ballmer. Ballmer emphasized the need to take risks and embrace failure as part of the process. He is quoted by the Wall Street Journal as saying, "The thing that separates the people who are successful from those who aren't is the willingness to take risks and make mistakes. We learn from our mistakes, and we keep moving forward." At Microsoft's leadership development conferences he would emphasize this message to attendees.

Derrick made thousands of decisions as the leader of the BING Team developing Microsoft's new search engine. Many didn't work out in the way he expected, which may seem surprising given the length of his tenure as the team leader for some of Microsoft's most public projects. One of his biggest failures was an investment in a new user experience for the browser Bing. As he describes, "I led the charge to introduce a new user experience on Bing. The result was a boost in user engagement, but it created a thirty million dollar loss that year. When I looked at the reason for the failure, I found one flaw in the layout for advertisements." After discovering the mistake, Derrick's team made a single change in the layout that was not visible to the eye. That one small difference turned things around and the following year his division not only recuperated the loss but generated fifty million dollars in revenue. Bing currently generates over ten billion dollars in revenue a year.

You might ask yourself why he didn't lose his job after making a thirty million dollar mistake. That is a fair question. The answer is because Derrick learned from his mistake and became a much better decision-maker because of it. Steve Ballmer, Bill Gates, and Satya Nadella all realize how critical it is to support risk-takers and to celebrate their failures as well as their successes. Ballmer didn't fire Derrick because he understood that Derrick was even more valuable to the company as the experience made him a much more savvy and resilient leader, traits that he would pass on to his team. He would not make the same mistake again, but a new hire might.

Investing in internal leaders who have failed intelligently can be a smart strategy for companies seeking growth and innovation. While it may seem counterintuitive, leaders who have experienced failure often possess valuable experience, resilience, and an adaptability that can benefit a company in the long run. The same goes for you, your children, friends, and colleagues. Encourage those around you to take risks and learn from failure. As a retiree try new things and begin to understand what you truly enjoy at this point in your life, as well as what you don't, and appreciate all of the challenges, joys, and mishaps that may come along with it. If you retire at sixty two and live until ninety two you have the same amount to time to live as from when you born to thirty, or thirty to sixty. That is a lot of time, get out there and make yourself uncomfortable. If you are mid-life, allow yourself and your partner to grow, change, evolve, take chances, and fail from time to time. Your lives will be richer for it. You both only have one life to live, make the best of it and let failure as well as success be your guide.

Throughout his career, colleagues have asked Derrick for advice on how they can achieve the same success at Microsoft he has had, often asking how they could get a job overseeing executives and working directly with the CEO. For many of these people this was one of their Core Twenty One, certainly in terms of their career. Yet there were two consistent challenges for senior managers who wanted to move up. They arise at every level of a company and both have to do with *Make Me Comfortable*. First, the majority of these executives were not comfortable admitting when their teams were not on schedule or needed help solving a problem. These were seasoned veterans but despite their extraordinary strengths the need to *Make Themselves Comfortable* became a career stopping Blind Spot. A CEO needs clear and honest assessments if the company is to succeed, and the management team needs to provide that. The second challenge was that the same skills that had made them successful so far were not the skills necessary to move up to the next level. The decision to develop new skill sets and let go of management styles that had helped them rise through the company was not an easy one for most people to make. *Make Me Comfortable* was hard at work as most of these executives did not want to take the risk, learn new skills, and reconsider *Who Am I* and *Who Can I Be*. By holding on to *Make Me Comfortable* they built ceilings over their careers that were difficult to break though without personal and professional growth.

The same applies in your career and everyday life. Upon graduation you may think that your growth is done and the world owes you for the time that you have already put in, but school is just the beginning. You have an amazing life of hard work and learning ahead if you want to be successful and achieve your Twenty One. If you are mid-life and feeling stuck you may find that you have limited your life or career by building a ceiling that can only be broken through by challenging yourself to grow and change. Your strengths may only get you so far, you will then need to develop new skills or find ways to apply your current skill set in a new manner. If you just retired, you may still be defining yourself as the former banker, car dealer, or baker and find it hard to learn new skills or have new experiences, so you stop trying. In each of these instances, *Make Me Comfortable* is at work slowing you down and removing possibilities.

Relationships, hobbies, and everyday challenges will require asking yourself the same questions as you would for your career. Are you standing in the way of your own success? If so, how and why? How much of your frustration is due to *Making Yourself Comfortable* or other Blind Spots? If you want to reach your Twenty One, you need to take chances, learn, grow, fail, and allow yourself to change for the better. It has been said that being comfortable is the enemy of progress, that is certainly true. Risk-taking is essential to success and innovation. It is difficult to introduce change into your life when you are feeling too comfortable in your knowledge, personal life, and career. Time passes far too quickly. If you wait to take the first steps, opportunities will pass you by.

Having never attended university themselves, Hugh Williams's parents wanted him to go to school and become a doctor. The problem was Hugh wasn't a great student. He was a bit lazy and preferred to spend time hanging out and playing music, so he didn't get into medical school. Disappointed, his parents suggested he become a pharmacist to which he replied, "OK, then that's what I'll do." *Make Me Comfortable* and *Who Am I Supposed To Be* were definitely at work.

Before heading to college Hugh took a year off to live in Indonesia. When he returned home he realized that he couldn't spend his life working in a pharmacy, so he changed his major from pre-med to computer science, a single step that changed his entire life. After graduation he was hired by a large Australian telecom and launched his own consulting business in tech. A few years later a professor from his university called to say that he had research funds to pay a PhD student to help develop a DNA and protein database as part of a research project he was working on. Hugh said yes to the job, which meant enrolling in school and getting his PhD as well. He worked hard, finishing the degree in three years with the belief it would make him more employable, but he soon realized that was not the case. He had become a highly qualified academic researcher but was hardly prepared to manage a team at a company, the job he was really interested in. Thankfully his university made him a job offer and he became a lecturer, writing academic papers and teaching.

Over the next ten years, Hugh rose to Associate Professor and, though his academic career was going well he could not shake his desire to work in tech. At that point Google called and asked if he would consider working for them. Soon to be married off he flew to Mountain View, California to meet with the company's founders. Working for Google would have meant moving from Australia to California, so he asked if they would give his fiancée a job as well and they said yes. He returned home with a job offer from Google that would allow his future wife to continue her career as well. It seemed the ideal opportunity for the couple.

At that point *Make Me Comfortable* took over. The company had offered reasonable pay but not enough to get a nice apartment in San Francisco. Equally important, Google was still a young company at that point and a number of search companies were going broke at the time. As Hugh described, "I thought, I'm going to basically drain my savings to work for a company that has no prospects. This doesn't seem like a very good idea for a guy who's about to get married and thinking about starting a family. And I thought the stock options Google was offering were probably worthless." Though his wife wanted to go to San Francisco, Hugh enjoyed their lifestyle and friends in Australia. He didn't want to take a risk and leave that all behind. He was just too comfortable. So he passed on the opportunity to become about the fiftieth employee at Google and what would have turned out to be a billion dollar payday.

Derrick too had the chance to work for Google early in his career. They approached his boss at Microsoft and said they wanted to hire her entire London-based team. She didn't feel comfortable making the decision for everyone, so they put it to a vote. By a result of four to three they decided to stay at Microsoft. That group did not want to risk change either and another potential billion dollar payday passed. Of course, neither Derrick nor Hugh knew of the potential windfall at the time, but that is how life works sometimes. They could have let that decision create doubt in their minds or cripple their careers, but they stayed focused and went on to be quite successful, living an ever evolving Twenty One. Having long term regret over things that did not work out is a losing game. You can't let the past hold you back, it will only be an emotional anchor that keeps you from taking the next steps forward.

As we have seen, when you find yourself saying *Make Me Comfortable* it may be time to reconsider your perspective. Working toward any of your Twenty One will require you to expand your comfort zone and that is a good thing. This may be as straightforward as setting aside a couple of hours a week to take a class, finding twenty minutes to exercise each day, or something more demanding like starting your own business or spending time living in another country. Whatever your objective, the happiness and fulfillment brought about by taking on new challenges and achieving your goals will bring its own form of comfort and satisfaction.

A lack of motivation does not only come from being complacent or living in a comfortable environment. You can become comfortable in a difficult or toxic situation as well. Challenges in life, work, and relationships can be overwhelming, wearing down a positive perspective and the ability to manifest change. We often begin to accept the conditions we find ourselves in because we are exhausted, afraid, or do not feel empowered to change them. Acceptance is a powerful coping mechanism. Over time you may find yourself making excuses for the situation you're in, normalizing it in the process. Once you begin to accept a negative environment as normal it becomes increasingly difficult to create positive change in your life. Saying, "That's just the way it is." gives away your power. Even when things are hard, know that you can and will find a way out.

When in a toxic relationship or environment you may find yourself thinking that everything is your fault, that you are not good enough to find another job, be respected, or deserving of a relationship in which you can be intimate and are treated well. Perhaps you begin to believe that good things simply do not exist in your life, or you are not empowered to make changes. People around you and online may reinforce these beliefs, further eroding your ability to bring about change and improve your situation. Toxic situations can seem overwhelming, which is exactly what the people creating those situations want you to feel. Individuals, organizations, educational institutions, and companies that manifest a toxic environment want you to feel disempowered, to believe that you are not able to move forward, grow, or succeed without them. If these are the messages that you are receiving, then it is time to move on and leave the dysfunction behind. Remove those people or organizations from your life and take the first step toward your Twenty One with the knowledge that you deserve better in life. You deserve to be treated well and have the intelligence, talent, dignity, beauty, personality, and skills to build and live a life that is fulfilling.

Both men and women face situations in life that are undermining and abusive. Fear, embarrassment, a lack of confidence or self worth, and more, will keep people from reaching out to friends, family, support groups, or their *Stars* to get the help and support they need, but that is exactly the time you should do so. The power of a positive community that supports its members can be a source of strength and energy. Seek out communities that, like your *Pillars*, are there to unconditionally help you learn and grow, finding happiness in your evolution and success. When you find yourself in a challenging or toxic situation you need to slowly begin to take yourself and your life back. Even in moments when it seems like you are alone there are people in the world who will value you, your knowledge, your personality, and the contribution you make to life.

The first step in manifesting that change is changing how you view yourself. This can be difficult to do as it will mean recognizing and admitting the situation you are in. If you need to, stop and take a few minutes to honestly define where you are in life. As you do so be clear about who and what, including your Blind Spots, are holding you back. You don't need to share this with anyone, but it is important to be honest with yourself so that you can move forward. The next step is to find one thing that you can work toward that will change your life or environment for the better. This may be something as life changing as leaving a job or relationship, reaching out for help from a family member, friend, trained professional, or not for profit organization, or simply doing the research necessary to learn a new skill or find a supportive community. Only you can decide whether the first step you need to take is big or small, but once you decide to move forward, don't stop. Those who want to hold you back will work hard to do so, do not give in. Respect yourself, and find a job, relationship, or community that does the same.

Remember Cira and Pasang from Chapter Two? Their desire to dream and succeed in the face of negative messages from those around them was a powerful force. Some of those messages came from people who believed a woman should only have a life that was deemed socially and culturally acceptable by the families and communities in which they lived. Pasang was told by family and friends in her Nepalese mountain village that a girl should not become a mountaineer or guide. Later she was pressured to stop the career she had worked so hard to build, something that brought her deep happiness. Cira had grown up in the polite society of the Southern United States and those around her did not believe that being a photographer or a mountaineer was an appropriate path for a girl. She persevered, not only becoming a photographer and award winning film maker, but the first American born woman to ascend Kanchenjunga, the world's third highest mountain at 28,169 feet. Had either woman decided to make those around them comfortable they would never have had the life changing fulfillment of achieving their goals. With each step along their paths, they overcame the silence in which they had hidden their dreams, growing stronger personally and in their careers. In doing so they became inspirations for young girls around the globe.

Even though both women were focused on exploring their personal goals, a deep seated desire to help others was central to their personalities as well. In 2013, they joined a series of medical treks in Nepal. Pasang worked as a translator and Cira documented the important work being done by doctors providing medical care in the remote mountain regions of Gorkha and Dolpa. Pasang not only translated during these clinics, but offered a compassionate bridge between two cultures, those of the Nepali villages and the internationally diverse members of the medical team.

In April 2015, an earthquake struck the region and both women supported the effort to repair and rebuild villages that were affected. Pasang was in a small village near Everest basecamp when the earthquake hit. She and her colleagues survived the enormous cloud of snow that rolled down the mountain and then set off through the treacherous snowpack to help those at basecamp an hour away. Once back in Kathmandu, Pasang began to mobilize the relief effort and with Cira's support was able to purchase tarps and other supplies for those who had lost their homes. Much of their effort was concentrated in the stone villages around Gorkha, especially Laprak where the quake had wiped out all of the village's six hundred homes. Cira sold a limited edition book of her photographs from the region to raise money for the relief effort. Pasang's personal achievements along with her selfless acts after the earthquake earned her the honor of being one of National Geographic's 2016 Adventurers of the Year.

The desire to help others is inherent in Cira and Pasang's lives and in their Twenty One Summers.

Moving beyond your personal comfort zone or those of your family and community is frequently viewed as a selfish pursuit. Know that you have the right to do so and to find personal fulfillment and happiness as you do. We are far too rarely told this in life. We sacrifice with good intent for family, friends, work, and community, but there is honor in taking care of yourself as well. Respect yourself and ask others to respect you too, doing so will be empowering. In Cira and Pasang's case, moving past those who doubted them and stepping outside of *Make Me Comfortable* has allowed them to achieve goals they could not have imagined when they began their journeys. They have enjoyed adventure and personal fulfillment while helping and inspiring others along the way.

You might think that given their strength and success, Pasang and Cira would be able to take on the world without question or concern. Yet, after years working together in the mountains, both women found themselves at a crossroads. For Pasang, the uncertainty surrounding the balance between home and career moved to the forefront of her life. She and her husband had a beautiful son and she was facing questions from her community and family regarding whether she should continue to climb. If people felt it was inappropriate for a girl to be a mountaineer they certainly questioned whether a mother should do so. Pasang was unsure of her decision as well. Mountaineering can be dangerous and meant a lot of time away from home. Was she putting herself and her family at risk by continuing to climb and guide others? How would her traveling affect her son's upbringing? Was it fair to be away for work? Despite her husband's mother living in the same home and helping with childcare the pressure mounted to stop doing the things she loved. During the same time Cira's life was rocked by a series of unexpected family related difficulties that caused her to pause and question.

At that point, a friend encouraged Cira to put together a short documentary titled *Dream Mountain*, an award-winning film that followed Pasang during a pivotal crux in her life and career. Cira had never made a documentary movie before nor taken on the challenge of producing and overseeing the creation of a high-altitude film. Could she make the shift from still photography to producing a movie? Would she be able to manage a full crew at high altitude? Equally important, nobody on the crew knew whether Pasang was ready to climb again now that she was a mother. As the team waited for her answer, Pasang traveled with her son and husband to the crew's base camp at Cholatse, a 6,400-meter (21,100 foot) mountain in Nepal ready to summit the mountain. They cheered both women as Pasang summited the peak and Cira produced and photographed her first movie. Pasang had twice transcended family and cultural challenges, as well as her own doubts, while paving the way for other female Nepali climbers. *Dream Mountain* has been screened at festivals around the globe and its message of strength and hope is inspiring women worldwide, as are Pasang and Cira.

If you find yourself thinking that Cira and Pasang's story does not relate to you, that their goals were too grand, or you do not have the time or desire to travel the world or climb mountains, remember that many people face individuals and communities that want to stifle their dreams as their goals do not *Make Them Comfortable*. It doesn't matter whether you want to learn the piano or change the world, it all begins with believing in yourself and taking the first small steps toward your goal. For Cira, it was receiving her grandfather's camera. For Pasang, it was going out into the mountains of her village to climb and prove she belonged. As each woman achieved success in one phase of their lives it allowed them, and their *Pillars*, to imagine greater goals that took them to places beyond their imaginations. Despite their achievements, or in some instances because of them, others sought to hold them back and undermine their careers. They overcame each of these challenges, and you can too.

Both Pasang and Cira serve as examples of how small steps can lead to an unexpected life and the beauty, fulfillment, and humble respect gained as you achieve your goals. Step by step they moved past the questions and negative messages in their lives to find success and satisfaction. You may find fulfillment from picking up a camera, renovating a car, getting a promotion, learning to swim, knitting your first sweater, or any other number of achievements. Whatever you choose for your Twenty One it will require a similar process; making the decision to stop listening to the reasons you "cannot do it," stepping out of your comfort zone, and looking for a community, *Teacher*, *Mentor*, *Pillar* to support you along your path. Face your fears or the doubts of others, decide on your first move, and then step by step begin to make your dreams and desires happen.

Do not embrace excuses or let your current life become the ultimate obstacle. We can all come up with reasons not to make something happen, but if you are reading this book you want to make a change in your life, to value yourself and your time in a new way. You have the power to do so, it is time to own that power and take the first steps away from *Make Me Comfortable* and toward a more fulfilling life.

Chapter Four
Yes, But Who Am I Really

Learning who you are is an evolutionary process, not only do we change but life changes around us. As you refine your Twenty One Summers and begin to understand the Blind Spots at work in your life, part of that change will be how you view yourself and your place in the world.

Over the first three chapters you have learned that personal evolution is not a singular event but a series of steps small and large that equal positive change in your life. This may include growing spiritually, intellectually, in terms of your personal life, on your career path, or in other ways. At this point in the book you may already be developing a new perspective. Perhaps the questions you are asking yourself and your friends have changed slightly, or you are feeling a bit more hopeful, open-minded, motivated, and empowered. You might find yourself thinking about your goals and the possibilities in life in new ways, or maybe you have done some research on a class, learned a new skill, or are looking into a trip that you have always thought about. Each of these are signs of personal growth, the beginning of a new definition of you. The next step is to use that newfound definition as a stepping-off point toward your Twenty One Summers and the next phase in your evolution.

Before you start you need a better understanding of where you are now, and this begins with *Yes, But Who Am I Really.* Most people define who they are with obvious choices such as mother, wife, daughter, mechanic, father, husband, son, nurse, athlete, gamer, artist. These are all important parts of *Yes, But Who Am I Really*, but they are titles that we give ourselves or are representative of things we do. Defining yourself solely by your titles is one of your Blind Spots. To really get to *Yes, But Who Am I Really*, we want you to move beyond these titles and dig a little deeper.

Stop for a moment and think about how you do each of the things that comprise your titles. Are you dedicated, hardworking, caring, procrastinating, giving, selfish? Do you always complete a task or let it drift? Are you the person people count on to make things happen or when they are in a time of need? Perhaps you are quietly supportive at home, work, play, and in your community. At work your strength might be group projects or maybe you prefer to work individually. Some people are data and technology oriented and love to dig into the details, while others have stronger conceptual or people skills. The world needs people of every flavor and what may seem like the smallest role can be important.

When I was President of the New York Chapter of the American Society of Media Photographers, one of our board members asked why another person was still on the board. "They don't do anything," he proclaimed. My response was this person was always positive during our board meetings and whenever we had a public event they always picked up the chairs and ice. Few of us had a car in New York and logistics were a challenge. Ice, chairs, accountability, and a good attitude may not have sounded like a lot to this board member, but to me they were priceless attributes. We didn't all need to be visionaries or leaders, a group can only function well when all the necessary roles are filled. This was not a matter of one role being better than another, each role is different and they are all equally important.

Of course, your *Yes, But Who Am I Really* shifts in different contexts. The person who brought ice to our events had a full life and successful career outside of the organization. Who you are at work or when speaking with a client is most likely not who you are at home, with friends and family, or when getting together with a group or club. You will be more private and protective in some situations and more open and vulnerable in others. In some ways, there are many versions of who you are to the world, and when done in a healthy way that is normal.

At this point we are asking you to look at all of those versions of yourself put together into one. Maybe a better way of saying it is to ask who you are beneath those external roles and titles. Why do you do what you do? What compels you to be a good mother or father, to exercise hard, to learn and take on new projects, to procrastinate, get in the way of your success, or to want to change your life for the better?

While descriptive terms such as mother, lawyer, or football player are comfortable to use and may represent things that are very important to us in life, they keep us from truly examining who we are and how we function in the world. Taking the time to understand what drives you is as important as knowing your Blind Spots and how they may be holding you back. The things that motivate you provide insight into why you make the choices you do. They also speak to how you view the world and are connected to your Twenty One Summers.

Ask yourself, are you motivated, considerate, idealistic, realistic, hardworking, procrastinating, inspirational, negative, supportive, disciplined? What drives and inspires you? Are you motivated by security, money, peace of mind, safety, legacy, fame, happiness, need, pride, love, hurt, injustice, family, friends, fear, praise, respect, personal history, career, travel, knowledge, talent, learning, adventure, the need to be heard, or something else? What are the secret things that you want to do or desire that you don't tell others? Secrets don't have to be negative, they can be positive things about yourself, your life, and your dreams. We are often afraid to say our secrets out loud for fear of others' responses, but the simple act of admitting them to yourself is empowering.

My mother and father would have said their motivation in life was their family and children, giving us a good life and opportunities when we grew up. It is hard to disagree with being a good mother or father, but I have wondered what it was in each of their lives that gave them that urgency, that goal. One that I am deeply thankful for. Being a good parent and taking care of their children was an outcome, a result of something that motivated them. Their answer might have been, "Because you are my son and I love you." I believe that. Yet there are many people who are not good parents. They are not kind, supportive, compassionate, or loving, for whatever reason they do not show up. So what was at the root of my parents' drive? Was it an especially good childhood, a difficult one, their own successes or failures, opportunities they did not have? These are questions that did not cross my mind when I was younger and I now will never be able to ask. You and I can ask ourselves what our motivations are though, whether we are talking about being a parent, how we choose our Twenty One Summers, or another part of life.

When looking at your initial list of motivations reflect on whether what you are describing is a Core Motivation, one of the things that drives many of your decisions. Why are you motivated to do the things you do, both good and bad? When are you able to show discipline in your life and when do you find it hard to stay focused? What knowledge, Blind Spot, or experience is driving your choices? Are they truly your choices or are they driven by external pressures? It is like the students in New York when we first discussed time and Twenty One Summers. I wondered why they were in my class and what they imagined their life would be once they graduated. Why did they choose that college and degree? Was it their decision? What was their motivation? Had they considered how their choices and motivations fit into their vision for life and their first list of Twenty One Summers?

Yes, But Who Am I Really is not only defined by the things that you do, but also by the things you can't or won't do. I am not a good singer, and though I love baseball and soccer I am past the point that I could ever play professionally. I could never run fast or far either. These are things that I am not, titles and descriptions that will never apply to me. I am dyslexic and never considered myself a good writer growing up, neither did my teachers. In fact, one English teacher in college was so concerned that he took me aside to discuss my lack of writing skills. In the end, I have written three books, including Twenty One Summers, but he was right I wasn't a good English student. Thankfully I have overcome some of those challenges and you can too. There is nothing wrong with not being good at something, we all have our strengths and weaknesses. Embrace your strengths, celebrate them, and build your life upon them if you can. Becoming obsessed with your weaknesses is a Blind Spot, it keeps you from focusing on the things that can make a positive difference in your life. Work on your weaknesses of course, but as you will see later in the book, time is better spent focusing on your talents, not mourning what you cannot do well.

Another part of your self-description, your *Yes, But Who Am I Really*, are your personal aspirations and who you would like to become personally and professionally, your Twenty One Summers. It is natural to try to create perfectly planned long term goals and exact definitions of success when defining *Yes, But Who Am I Really* and where your Twenty One will take you. Like my friend JC, you might want to design your own guitar. From there you may want to become the world's leading bespoke guitar maker, with accolades from the world's greatest guitarists and all the fame and happiness that comes with that success. In your imagined Twenty One you will live in a house near the ocean in Manhattan Beach, California, have a studio to make guitars in your home and only do special orders for guitarists whose music you respect. While in Los Angeles, you will find a partner who is also into music and will surf with you during your downtime. Your dog will be named Jerry and you will all hang together as you walk the boardwalk and eat tacos at your favorite taco stand. These are a great series of goals. It is good to have clarity in terms of what you desire and to be able to visualize it as well, but you also want to be flexible in terms of where your guitar dreams take you.

Would it be a disaster if your guitar making took you to Nashville or Berlin instead of Los Angeles, and your partner, though very supportive, was into hiking and knitting instead of surfing? What if you made bespoke guitars for a range of artists, or if a company in Miami asked you to make a line of high-end bespoke guitars that they co-branded with you? Would that be a negative outcome? You could rigidly hold onto your initial vision and force your way to Los Angeles, or you could allow yourself to be flexible following unimagined opportunities as they arise, letting life treat you well in ways you couldn't have known when you made your initial list.

It is important to have a clear vision of where you would like each of your Twenty One to take you, but instead of an exact definition of success imagine the direction you want to go in terms of life, career, and relationships, and leave the pathway open and flexible. Allow the lessons you learn along the way to influence your path and inform your decisions. You may end up in a slightly different place in life, but what a great place it might be. Don't be afraid to learn, adjust, and evolve along the way. The ability to do so is truly one of life's great beauties. Begin by clearly defining the first step you will take on this journey as that first step is important, then respond to the challenges and blessings along the way. You will be much happier and perhaps, like Derrick and me, truly surprised at the outcome.

A great analogy for taking a well defined first step and being flexible during the process comes from Derrick's world of software development. Like you, software developers have options for setting and reaching goals. Some are more defined and linear in their process while others allow for the integration of input from outside sources, adjust to new opportunities, and include lessons learned along the way. The later model is a model called the Agile Process. This is an iterative and collaborative approach that emphasizes incremental delivery, team collaboration, and continual planning and learning.

The Agile Process begins with an initial vision of the final product or outcome but is flexible enough to incorporate new information and lessons learned throughout the process. It fosters innovation by encouraging experimentation and integrating feedback from potential customers and the company's business team on an ongoing basis. This means that the final outcome may be different than originally imagined, which is part of Agile's strength. The process reduces risk and increases the chance for success by delivering results early and often, usually in weeks as opposed to months or years. Most of the software you use today is built using the Agile Process, including apps and programs for companies such as Uber, Google, Instagram, and TikTok. It is essential for these companies to have a strong long term vision, but it is equally important to be able to quickly adapt to shifts in the marketplace.

Prior to Agile most software was designed using what is called the Waterfall Process. In this model a linear approach to project management follows a series of steps in sequential order. Each stage must be completed before initiating the next phase. The key to this model is setting a very precise and clearly defined outcome at the beginning of the project, with everyone working toward that predetermined goal.

The Waterfall Process provides an easy to understand structure with identifiable milestones for each phase of the process. However, it also has drawbacks such as a lack of flexibility to meet changing requirements, delayed feedback from customers or users, high risk of failure, and an inability to make changes if errors are found late in the process. The lack of flexibility is a huge problem with this model. The world and technology are constantly evolving and it is quite possible that the development team's clearly defined view of the world when starting may not be true once the project has been completed. In fact, the world may have changed significantly over the course of the design process.

An example of this was Windows software the world's largest software platform for PCs in the early 2000s. Windows Vista was developed over the course of five years, with the final version released on January 30th, 2007. Between 2001 and early 2007, two groundbreaking disruptions occurred. Just weeks before the software was released, the first iPhone was announced. So the same month Windows Vista was launched as a desktop-only software the world was introduced to smartphones. Vista did not work with iPhones, nor could it be quickly adapted to allow for the integration of mobile apps or devices. It was in essence years behind on the day it was launched. The second disruption was the launch of Facebook, introducing social media to the world and changing the way people interacted forever. Once again, due to using the Waterfall Process and a rigid linear vision Windows was unable to respond to this change and was left years behind.

It is important to note that there are times when the Waterfall Process is necessary to develop repeatable processes that give predictable high quality outcomes. Brain surgeons and pilots are two examples of professions where their practitioners need to follow a clear structure with identifiable milestones during each phase of the process. There may be room for responding to unexpected situations that arise, but in general you want people in each of these professions to follow a repeatable process that will give consistent high quality outcomes. There are other instances when the Waterfall Process makes sense as well, such as payroll and banking, but it is problematic when applied to life and the unexpected changes that take place.

Take a moment and consider how you problem solve. Which process are you applying as you work toward your Twenty One? If you stay agile, you will be able to integrate new experiences, input from other sources, and lessons learned along the way. If you approach life with the Waterfall Process, holding rigidly on to the pathway laid out when you took your first step, it will be difficult to respond to the challenges and opportunities that life brings. Derrick and I have both found the Agile Process to be more fruitful as it allows you to set a goal, focus on the first step, adapt to change, and incorporate what you learn from new experiences, resources, and communities, while refining your vision as you go.

Going back to JC's guitar story, perhaps you wanted to be the world's leading guitar maker but found that you are much better at making cellos, violins, and other types of musical instruments. If that is the case, it may be time to adjust your Twenty One and become the world's best known bespoke cello and violin maker. Equally important, you may learn that you don't enjoy guitar making. Learning what you don't like is as important as learning what you like to do. Let your vision change to reflect the growth in your talent and experience, that makes it possible to pivot into something new. Experiment, it's your life, live it.

There are times when it can be difficult to move from who you are to who you want to be. Some of your apprehension may come from the Blind Spots *Who Am I, Who Am I Supposed To Be, Who Can I Be, Yes, But Who Am I Really,* and *Make Me Comfortable.* As we have seen, the ability to improve your life can be stifled by how you define yourself and the messages you have heard growing up and as an adult. Local belief systems, communities, and family may be supportive, but may also hinder your progress.

In order to reach your personal and professional goals, you have to be willing to overcome the fear and apprehension that many people associate with change and let go of habits and lifestyles that may be making you comfortable. You are not alone if you fear the unknown or have been living life the same way for so long that you cannot imagine anything different. Some of us are still living by the same rules, motivations, guidelines, and beliefs that made us comfortable as children. We solidified these ways of thinking as we moved through our teen years and perhaps as young adults. They may have served us well during those years but have now become Blind Spots that keep us from evolving. Life and the world around us can change in unimaginable ways and you need to grow along with them.

There will be times in your life when your belief systems and ways of thinking no longer fit the life you are living or the person you have become. In those moments, you need to reconsider your Twenty One and begin the Agile Process. It will be time to incorporate new knowledge and perspectives as you review *Yes, But Who Am I Really*. Strive to be flexible as you refocus energy and work toward new goals. Move through your fear and have faith in yourself and your future.

For many, *Yes, But Who Am I Really* becomes a question that they ask themselves regularly, checking in to see if they are on track to become the person they hope to be and if their Twenty One are aligned with their motivations. These people adjust their course in small increments, working to improve the areas of need that become apparent. For them, growth is like a ship whose direction needs slight adjustments as it sails to its destination. They raise and drop anchor as they need to learn, grow, or rest a bit. Processing change takes time and though you never stop learning, it is important to give yourself time to rest, reflect, enjoy, and cherish your successes.

Stop and enjoy, but do not linger too long as it may inhibit your progress. Derrick and I have both found that friends and acquaintances have stopped growing at various points in their life with many never getting started again, and others not realizing they had stopped until years had passed. Sometimes people stop because they believe they should, other times because they feel they have achieved a certain goal or level of success. Many people stop growing after they graduate from high school, others after college or when they get married. Then there are people who stop when they have children or reach a certain point in their career. All of these are seminal moments in life and can be very satisfying. Taking the time to adjust makes sense, but after a while you may ask yourself how much time has passed, what happened to your drive, and why you aren't feeling satisfied anymore. I have listened to a number of friends, colleagues, and clients question when and how they stopped growing personally or professionally. This can happen while in school, as an empty nester, during retirement, or any time in between. Time is so very valuable, don't take it or your life for granted.

As you achieve your goals, keep moving forward you will thank yourself for it later. It is like being a surfer, as you ride each wave you are always looking for the next one. At some point every wave hits the shore and every ride comes to an end, no matter how good the ride. So don't rest when something goes well; use it as a stepping stone toward what you want to achieve next. For instance, if you get your first exhibition as an artist, gig as a musician, or job coding with a tech firm, that event alone won't change your life. You need to use that success to ride the next wave, to step up to the next level of your job or find the next good thing and make it happen. Time moves quickly, so get that master's degree or learn to snowboard, a year or two is going to pass either way. At the end of those two years you can either feel the satisfaction of having achieved something new or wonder why your life hasn't changed for the better.

In the end, the question is how and why you are improving your life, or not. Is your *Yes, But Who Am I Really* helping you reach your Twenty One or holding you back and limiting your possibilities? Because while life may get in the way sometimes, it does for all of us, how you address the moments when things are challenging goes a long way toward defining who you are. Never give up, never stop exploring, don't let the difficult times win. Life doesn't always work seamlessly, but why shouldn't you have some of the same expectations of success in your life that tech firms do for their projects? We know that an agile and flexible approach to your Twenty One is beneficial, so define yourself clearly, understand what motivates you, integrate new knowledge and experiences, and work toward a life that will bring you happiness and self-satisfaction.

Being clear about your beliefs, habits, and motivations is important. Take a few minutes and contemplate which thoughts, habits, motivations, individuals, communities, and beliefs are moving you toward your goals. Now list the things that may be hindering you. Be honest with yourself. Work to remove rigidity and chaos from your life and bring an agile, streamlined, way of thinking to your daily routine. Doing so will keep life interesting, and you engaged with the beauty and magic of the world from before graduation until long after retirement.

As I have moved through life, my *Yes, But Who Am I Really* has changed substantially, at times without my being aware of it and other times due to personal choices or unexpected events. Each shift presented its own challenge becoming an important identity shaping lesson along the way, hopefully one well learned.

Growing up in a small town I felt the security of being much like everyone else. Of course our families were not all the same and we all had different interests, but at its core our town was a quiet farm town and suburb. Hard work, family, going to school, treating each other well, leaving the world a better place than you found it, and making something better for yourself in life were valued. You were radical if you wore different clothes or had a haircut that wasn't like everyone else's. My parents told me to explore, to try sports, musical instruments, books, camping, and other things to see what I liked and didn't. This helped lead to a lifetime of exploration. Outside of the same questions most children and teenagers have about life, their bodies, whether they fit in, and their performance in school or other activities, my *Yes, But Who Am I Really* was rather well defined. Life, the town, people's lifestyles, and the general beliefs were consistent.

Once I left for college I was in for a big surprise, first at a small college in the Midwestern United States and then at a major university. I found myself uncomfortable with one situation that was more confining and a bit overwhelmed by another that was large, diverse, and in which you had complete freedom. Living without the ability to define *Yes, But Who Am I Really* based on those around me brought challenges. Looking outward, I didn't feel as though I fit in at either the college or university. Everyone seemed more engaged and as if they were secure with their career and place in things. I thought that I should have an answer for what I wanted to be in life and a Waterfall Process based five year plan to get there. Though I wasn't aware of it at the time one of my biggest challenges was not others, but myself. I hadn't yet developed the ability to define my *Yes, But Who Am I Really* for myself. It was time to learn what my Core Values were, to explore in new ways, make mistakes, and grow.

Much of the discomfort that I experienced was due to personal growth and learning who I was in each of the situations that came along, whether that was being exposed to a new course of study, lifestyle, way of thinking, economic differences, rules, or social situation. Some of the people from the small college have become lifelong friends, but it was there that I truly understood that I did not want to continue living the small town lifestyle I had grown up in. Though others found comfort in a town or school where everyone knew one another I longed for a place where I could explore, risk-take and grow with a certain amount of anonymity. Doing the same job in the same town or region for the rest of their life was exactly what many at both schools aspired to, while I felt uncomfortable knowing what I would be doing for the next five years, not to mention the next fifty. I have never been good at answering "What do you see your life like in five years?" or "What is your plan for the next five years?" Wanting either a consistent and well defined future or one that reveals itself over time are both valid choices. Think of it as the Waterfall versus Agile Process. Understanding which kind of person you are as you define and explore your Twenty One will be helpful.

The uncertainty I faced at the larger university was just the first round of training for working and surviving in new, challenging, diverse situations. When moving to Los Angeles, I didn't really know anyone in the city or understand the differences between there and where I grew up. The people were different, the values were different, and the way business was handled was different, but I slowly established myself, learned how things worked, and began to understand *Yes, But Who Am I Really* in a completely different environment. The same thing occurred when moving to New York. I didn't know anyone there either and had only met people in the photography world during trips to the city to promote my work. New York seemed like a beast. Fast paced and densely packed, it could not have been more different than Los Angeles, but that beast slowly became my best friend and by embracing the Agile Process it allowed my *Yes, But Who Am I Really* to change in ways that I never would have dreamed of.

At this point you might be thinking that I am comfortable making these moves. Perhaps, that I am outgoing and it is easy for me to be social and meet people in a new city. That is not the case. Each new place was a personal and professional challenge. Sometimes you have to go out into the world feeling unsure of yourself in order to bring change and opportunity into your life. The desire to test my skills and see what life could become was more important than my apprehensions. I am hardly an extrovert, but I do enjoy the excitement brought by new experiences as well as the satisfaction of reaching one of my Twenty One. I reached many of my Twenty One during the time in New York, more than I could have ever imagined. It was both hard work and exhilarating; the time there changed me and is one reason this book exists.

The university that I taught at included one of the country's leading design schools. Almost every student who arrived had been the best photographer, designer, or artist at the school in their hometown. Now they had moved to New York and were in a class filled with people who were also the best in their hometown. Their identity, their *Who Am I*, was immediately turned upside down. To make the challenge harder, they needed to integrate who they were at home into a diverse multicultural institution in the middle of one of the world's most challenging cities. All while immersing themselves in a curriculum that asked them to grow at every turn. It was an exciting time in each student's life, but also a challenging one for many. Some went through multiple iterations of *Yes, But Who Am I Really,* while others found their footing more quickly. As you can imagine from my story about graduation, my focus was on getting students ready for life after school and giving them the best possible opportunity to succeed. You only have so much influence as an educator, so each individual's drive, motivation, talent, focus, and ability to evolve plays a large role in what they learn and who they became while at a university.

What those students faced going to design school in New York was similar in some ways to what an athlete faces when competing nationally for the first time. At home, each athlete is the best in their city, they win regularly and enjoy success. Upon arrival at the National Championships they are suddenly one of many talented athletes. Losing may be new to many of these competitors and how they handle that reality is essential. If they let it discourage them their career as an athlete could be over, and for some it may affect the rest of their lives. If they can understand and accept this change with the same fierce drive that they compete with, their *Yes, But Who Am I Really* will become stronger and they will be able to use the experience to propel themselves to even higher levels in sports and life.

Derrick had a similar experience moving up the ladder at Microsoft. You would think that it was easy for him, but each step was a personal challenge. At every level he felt out of place. The competition was intense and with each move he had to learn and apply new skill sets with new teams. He was hardly an expert when he started a new position at the company, but over time he became one. When you find yourself in a situation like this strive to be comfortable with the fact that you are not an expert, or at least not yet. You don't have to prove that you're the best right away. Take advantage of the opportunity to expand your experience, skill set, and understanding of your strengths and weaknesses. That alone will move you forward in your life and career.

Be sure to check in on yourself and your *Yes, But Who Am I Really* along the way. Remember that perfection isn't achievable and is often the enemy of growth and evolution. Keep this in mind as you strive to create change in your life.

Kodo Nishimura is an example of someone who has constantly questioned the definition of *Yes, But Who Am I Really* in an effort to find personal happiness and help others do the same. The humble lifestyle of a Buddhist monk hardly belies the life of Kodo, whose focus, compassion, and a love for beauty, make-up, and fashion have led him from a quiet life to becoming one of TIME Magazine's 2021 *Next Generation Leaders* and one of Japan's leading LGBTQ activists. The ability to reconcile this duality and utilize it for positive change has allowed Kodo to appear in an extraordinary range of venues, all with the goal of promoting acceptance. He has spoken at the United Nations Population Fund in New York, presented at Yale, given a talk with TEDx, been a guest on *Queer Eye: We're in Japan*, and been interviewed by CNN, BBC, and NHK in Japan, among numerous other news outlets and publications. Add this to his book *This Monk Wears Heels*, which is available in six languages, and a successful international career as a make-up artist overseeing a team at the Miss Universe Pageant and you find someone who is extraordinarily driven. Yet, Kodo's vision of who he is, his *Yes, But Who Am I Really*, has not always been so clear. He has often questioned his path as he worked toward, and redefined, his Twenty One.

The first time I met Kodo, he was a shy retiring student standing in a cool empty hallway at Parsons School for Design in New York. He dreamt of doing make-up for Miss Universe and wanted to join my fashion photography class to learn from the make-up artists that we collaborated with each week. During these classes he wondered aloud whether he would ever be considered beautiful given his features and Japanese heritage. The male models with whom we worked were more physically imposing and their features chiseled. Bound with insecurity but filled with belief in a goal that felt far out of reach, he deftly and unassumingly learned his craft, engaging the students and stylists who worked with us with equally high regard. As it turned out, a make-up artist for Miss Universe was giving a workshop in New York at that time and Kodo wrote to see if he could take the class as a biological man. The barrier to the course was not his identity but the cost, which was equal to one month's rent. Overwhelmed and confused he consulted with his mother who told him to invest in his future.

Kodo welcomed make-up as a form of personal expression. This was a step in his soon to be accelerated evolution and one of the first defining moments in his *Yes, But Who Am I Really*. "I learned that if you know how to express yourself, if you know what you have and know how to accentuate it, you can express who you are. This motivated me and it's why I wanted to learn make-up, so that I can feel like I'm OK." The genesis of his transformation did not come from this newfound confidence, but from a frightened Korean student who had to leave school to join the military. For his final assignment, the student arrived in class in his military uniform and performed the exercises and drills that were soon to become part of his life. Kodo said, "That stung my heart because he was usually quiet, but I could feel that he didn't want to leave school. He didn't want to join the military. I could feel his anger and determination and noticed his sorrow. Because he was showing his vulnerability, I realized that I have to face my vulnerability and show it to others if I want to touch other people." Once Kodo accepted the need to engage life openly he was able to face the world with a sense of grace that became central to his mission. Allowing himself to be honest and vulnerable was not an easy task as it was fraught with potential hurt and misunderstanding. At this point, he had not only begun to understand the Blind Spots that were holding him back, but also one of the first changes that needed to take place as he redefined his *Yes, But Who Am I Really*. Taking that step placed him on a path to a new life and empowered him to help others, one of his main goals.

Though it is at the core of his teaching today, Kodo had shunned Buddhism along with its rules and rituals as a child. His choice to return to the Temple of his childhood to become a monk was complicated by his feeling that Buddhism was incompatible with his gender fluid lifestyle. In New York, he had flourished: "I bought a lot of extravagant clothes, and was encouraged by my friends, colleagues and the environment, but I wasn't sure about becoming a monk because there is a set of rules that guide a monk's life. A monk cannot wear lavish clothes. A monk cannot even watch music or dance performances."

Kodo was facing questions many of us face as we begin to evolve. How do I reconcile who I am with who I want to be? How can I overcome the fear that may be associated with change? Am I willing to change my current lifestyle or perhaps lose some friends? How will I build my career during and after this change? Will my newfound beliefs alienate me from my current life? It would have been easy for him to give up, take the easy path, and embrace a life in which he was able to live openly while enjoying one of the world's greatest cities. The life that he had created could not have been easy to leave behind. As we now know, we too often embrace the safety and comfort of the familiar and those around us are often happiest when we define our lives by *Making Them Comfortable.*

Yet, Kodo understood that despite any concerns he might have he needed to go home and embrace this part of his past. "I had questions, and thought if I study to become a monk I may be able to become somebody more complete. What I learned during the monk training was that to evolve I had to face what I had been avoiding."

As his studies progressed, he was faced with numerous practices that required him to select his gender and manifest his identity. The increasing dissonance of these moments led him to request a meeting with the Master of the Temple. Nervously, Kodo asked whether becoming a monk would mean disavowing his lifestyle, to which the Master answered that the most important message of their denomination, Jodo-shu Buddhism, which means Pure Land Buddhism, is to tell everybody that we can be equally saved. If you are faithful, you can be saved, it's like moonlight. It is beaming onto everybody. As long as Kodo was able to deliver this message the Master did not see a problem. Kodo explained, "So your gender doesn't matter. Japanese monks can now get married and have different jobs and lifestyles. I felt like an anchor on my heart was lifted. I felt free. Maybe I can live true to who I am and become a monk and be confident."

It was at this moment Kodo realized that he needed to dedicate his life to helping others find the acceptance, freedom, and fortitude to be who they truly want to be. Providing insight into how to navigate the times when people felt conflict between their beliefs internally or with society, "I thought that the message that I had just received was too good to keep within me. I know that many people are struggling with limitations or expectations because of faith globally. Not only faith, but prejudice or cultural expectations are choking people when they're not supposed to choke them, because religion is supposed to help people." He went on to say, "I needed to share this message, not really to make people believe in Buddhism but to introduce bits of Buddhism. So, it's my mission to introduce them to this idea of equality in Buddhism and show that I'm happy being who I am, doing what I love." As part of this mission, Kodo is working to change laws to protect Japan's LGBTQ population and collaborating with global partners to bring a message of positive acceptance to a greater portion of the population. Though the LGBTQ community is central to Kodo's message, he is working on an international basis to help people of all ages and lifestyles find their strength and understand they have the power to be their authentic selves.

Many of us have the desire to help others and make the world a better place in big ways and small. We want to improve the lives of our family, partners and friends, or perhaps our local community. Others aspire to effect positive change on a national or international level, but it is difficult to truly help someone else until you have defined your *Yes, But Who Am I Really*. As we saw with Kodo, if we want to be effective, we need to first face the changes we need to make in ourselves and overcome our obstacles, fears, and preconceptions.

As you move through that process, you will become a stronger, more positive version of yourself, adjusting and clarifying your goals along the way. Even the oldest beliefs and traditions function differently over time. They may inform, but as the Master at Kodo's Temple showed, their application and interpretation often change as the world evolves. At each step along his path, Kodo achieved his goals, redefined them, and then moved past them. He continues to help others, most recently on a tour across Europe.

The truth is, over the course of your life there really isn't a single answer regarding who you are. It is who you are at that time in your life. Always take the time to appreciate the current version of yourself as you work toward your Twenty One Summers and like Kodo, evolve into the next version of you. Embrace every step of the pathway. Change isn't about waiting for the future, it is enjoying the process and being excited about the good things that happen along the way to reaching your goal.

I have goals of course, my Twenty One are well defined, but they too have changed as my life and *Yes, But Who Am I Really* have been redefined. In fact, this book is new to the Twenty One Summers of both Derrick and I. If we had not had long conversations while teaching and learning fashion photography the idea for this book never would have come about and we would not have collaborated.

The beauty of this project is that we come from different backgrounds in terms of our careers. Derrick had never written a book, while I had written two before our collaboration. He had extraordinary tech and corporate experience, while my strengths were in the arts and education. We both had spent a lifetime creating, but in very different environments. Once we were able to see the similarities in our creative and work experience it opened the door to defining the Blind Spots we saw at work in our lives and those of others. We talked about the value of time, our personal and career goals or Twenty One Summers, and then the idea for the book.

The minute we agreed to collaborate on this project our Twenty One Summers shifted. As we have delved into this new experience and learned from each other, our *Yes, But Who Am I Really* has changed as well. Despite long histories in our respective fields, writing Twenty One Summers was something completely new to us both. Now that the book is done, we are facing new challenges as individuals and as a creative team. Whether we will be successful or not is impossible to say. Without question, the pathway that we are on today would not exist if we had not been open to evolving personally and professionally. We had to be willing to move out of our comfort zones and take on something new.

You may feel similarly challenged when going to school, moving to a new city or country, taking on a new project, working in a new field, or joining a club and learning new skills. Stepping into situations where you are stretched and asked to move beyond your personal boundaries will always change how you view the world and the world views you. These times do not need to be stressful or upend your life. Just be yourself and embrace the possibilities those moments bring as well as how they will change *Yes, But Who Am I Really*. The pleasure and satisfaction of achieving a goal, big or small, can be extraordinary. Just be sure to check in on yourself along the way and adjust your Twenty One to match the person you aspire to be.

Chapter Five

Knowledge As A Wall

We are told that knowledge is the key to our growth and success, and it is, but in many cases it is also a barrier to our ability to grow and change personally, professionally, and as society. Though this may seem contrary to popular belief, it may be one of our biggest Blind Spots. Derrick and I see this regularly in the worlds of art and technology, but honestly this Blind Spot is at work in all of our lives daily.

Let me explain it this way. Imagine all of your knowledge in a single box. When you are young the box is small. As you move through life and read, study, spend time online, watch videos, travel, play, have new experiences, and learn from others, your knowledge grows and the boundaries of your box expand. The range of opportunities available to you expand as well, along with your understanding of what it may mean to choose one opportunity over another. Each time the *Walls of Your Knowledge* move farther out, your decision making process becomes more informed helping you make better choices and giving you greater insight into what your Twenty One might be.

So where is the Blind Spot? There are vast areas of knowledge outside of your personal life experience. If you only make decisions based on the knowledge and experience inside the *Walls of Your Knowledge* you will be excluding thousands of options. In essence, the *Walls of*

Your Knowledge are boundaries built around you, limiting you by virtue of what you know. These walls become a barrier to your growth and an important Blind Spot affecting your ability to create positive change. Small businesses, corporations, communities, and societies have their own walls too. Each is limited by the people who run or inhabit them and the culture they foster within.

As we learned in Chapter Two, the way that we define and interpret the world is largely shaped by our families, friends, teachers, colleagues, local communities, culture, and the environments in which we grow up. These influences also fill our box, helping build the boundaries that affect the way we interpret or apply the knowledge inside our walls and new knowledge and experiences that enter our lives. In many respects we understand and interpret everything locally, based on the knowledge and culture in which we reside. This is especially true during the first part of our lives.

Here is a simple example of how this works. Imagine a tall slender woman with long flowing black hair and a confident smile wearing a flowing dress that moves as she walks along a narrow winding street in Paris or Istanbul. Everyone reading this description will envision her differently, she will be a different ethnicity, wear a different dress, have a different build, hair style and make-up, or perhaps no make-up at all, and walk with a different kind of confidence. The buildings, look, and feel of the city street that each of you pictures will also be distinct. The woman's clothing or ethnicity might be similar to your local community or perhaps based on what you imagine someone in Paris or Istanbul looks like. How she moves through the street will be a reflection of your personal experience as well. There will be some similarities of course, but each of you will interpret this description based on where you reside, local beliefs, travel, education, social and economic factors, and a number of other customs and experiences that go into how we perceive a person or a situation.

Now imagine a man walking down the street. He has black hair and is wearing a white shirt with black pants and a belt. You can tell that he is deeply in thought as he walks. Where did you imagine the man? Was he in a town or city? In New York, Mumbai, Nepal, your hometown, a small village in Switzerland? Was the street paved, was there a sidewalk, or was it a dirt road? Were there trees, fields, buildings? Was he wearing a white t-shirt, formal oxford button down, a loose linen shirt with the top buttons unbuttoned? Were his pants slacks, chinos, maybe black jeans? What ethnicity was he? Was his hair short or long, straight or wavy? Was he looking down as he walked or looking up smiling? The possibilities are endless. What you imagined in both of these scenarios was defined by your experience and the *Walls of Your Knowledge*. Try this exercise with your book club, family, or group of friends and see how they describe the woman and man. Your similarities and differences in choices will be interesting.

The *Walls of Your Knowledge* can limit you at any point in your life. A student sitting in their apartment the day after graduation can only imagine the career paths and lifestyle choices they have been exposed to over the course of their lives. There are thousands of opportunities they may learn of during their career, or perhaps never hear about, thus limiting their choices in life. Parents who have just become empty nesters may find it challenging to imagine their next steps beyond the life that they have known for decades. They may struggle to redefine who they are and what their next Twenty One Summers will be. After forty years of work a retiree may not feel like they have many options, though this is not necessarily the case. The opportunities after retirement may be almost unlimited.

Once you get used to living within the *Walls of Your Knowledge* it can take a while to imagine or embrace opportunities outside of the lifestyle that you have become used to. If you are mid-career, you may not be able to fathom moving onto another career path or phase in life, believing your choices are limited. These beliefs can be frustrating. The phrase, "I feel like I'm up against a wall." might ring true. The walls that you are up against may be those of your knowledge and your inability to see past them.

Sometimes you have to take a leap of faith, trying things you do not fully understand. Your boundaries are there to break and you are far more empowered than you may believe. Ultimately, you can either accept the limitations of your knowledge or you can reach out, learn, expand your boundaries, and find new opportunities. The choice is yours.

Artists have been thinking beyond *Walls of Their Knowledge* for generations. In 1907 Picasso painted *Les Demoiselles d'Avignon*, a work that changed the idea of representation in the arts forever. Picasso and Braque created cubism, a way of representing reality that had not been seen in painting before they made the leap. Another example is Andy Warhol's creation of Pop Art which often focused on everyday objects like Campbell's Soup Cans. Warhol celebrated the everyday, often utilizing skills learned in his early commercial career to elevate the mundane to high art. The list of artists and other creatives who have moved past the *Walls of Their Knowledge* and changed the way we view art and life is long and diverse, beginning with the first people to draw on the walls of caves or create the first tools tens of thousands of years ago. Innovators, entrepreneurs, artists, musicians, writers, fashion designers, and others have been creating ever-changing interpretations of our life, culture, and the times in which we live. They consistently move beyond the *Walls of Their Knowledge* and society's expectations. You can do the same in your own life.

When I began my career as a photographer, I didn't have any formal training. The jobs were much harder than expected, so I decided to attend The Art Center College of Design in Pasadena to improve my skills. After graduation, the creative director of a local magazine asked if I was going to photograph fashion or portraits. She explained that fashion photographers are hired to take portraits, but portrait photographers are rarely asked to create fashion images. It was time to decide what direction my career would take, but the fashion industry was a mystery to me. I didn't know much about it other than what I had learned in photography class at school.

A few days after the conversation I called a model from San Diego to get more insight. She was going to walk in the fashion shows in Paris the following week and I asked if I could stay at the model's apartment there for a day and then head out on my own. She thankfully said yes. I certainly didn't know anything about Paris or Fashion Week and had only been out of the country one time prior, but I did know that being a fashion photographer was going to provide more options and a more interesting career than being a portrait photographer. So off I went with my bad French, best clothes, and almost no money. Each day I would dress in my nicest suit and go to the part of the Louvre where they were hosting the shows. For five days, I quietly waited outside the entrance and embarrassingly asked people in French if they had an extra ticket. After a few days the guards felt sorry for me and would bring me an espresso or water when they could. With little money left after school I could only afford the food from carts and small shops around the city. I learned to say "un sandwich au jambon et au fromage, s'il vous plait," "A ham and cheese sandwich, please." It was an inexpensive option, and I ate them every day until I could barely stand the sight of one.

A few people at fashion week were kind and I think others took pity on me and gave me tickets, so I was able to attend a number of shows including Valentino and Lagerfeld. Being in Paris led to attending fashion week events and getting to know other models, agencies, designers, and potential clients. It was all a bit nerve-racking, but it was the best lesson that I could have had. I learned about the art and business of fashion as well as styling, casting, and so much more. The results of my efforts were inspiring, they gave me the excitement and confidence to learn new things, create new work, and step into an industry that I was just beginning to understand. As the creative director tells the story, "One minute I'm asking him if he wants to shoot fashion, and the next week he's in Paris with Lagerfeld." It was hardly that easy. I was a small town boy from the Midwestern United States, which certainly isn't a bastion of French fashion, stepping into a world beyond my knowledge or imagination. The trip was a leap of faith, traveling to a city, a lifestyle, and profession that I knew little or nothing about. If I hadn't reached beyond the *Walls of My Knowledge* and attempted something completely new I never would have had the career that I have now and certainly wouldn't be sitting here writing this book today. The experience gave me confidence and taught me to cherish every success big and small. Living inside the *Walls of Your Knowledge* limits the possibilities in life. Many times, opportunities do not come twice.

A second example of stepping completely outside of the *Walls of My Knowledge*, and certainly not the last, was getting on a plane to Russia with two email addresses, my CV, and the six Russian words that I knew. This trip took place ten years after my first trip to Paris, but was no less daunting. I had visited Saint Petersburg for three days a few months prior and while there decided that I wanted to do one talk, lecture, exhibition, something, in Russia, but didn't have any idea how that would happen.

After returning from that first trip I ran into someone on a train platform in Philadelphia who had a bag that read US Embassy Moscow. I never talk to people on planes and trains, but went up to him and said that I would like to do one project in Russia. He gave me a little advice and his business card, so I emailed him a proposal. In return he sent me two email addresses, one in Moscow and one in Saint Petersburg. That first trip to Moscow, navigated with a hotel lobby guidebook map and the kindness of strangers, led to sixteen years of work with thirty two cultural, educational, and governmental organizations in twenty nine cities across Russia. Partners included The State Hermitage Museum, the United States Department of

State, The Moscow Youth Biennale, The Regional Government of Perm, the Pro Arte Foundation, The Trust for Mutual Understanding, and multiple branches of the National Museum of Contemporary Art, among others. Each step along the way was an act of hard work, trust, and faith that led me on extraordinary adventures across the country. I have tried many things in life, this is one that went from seemingly impossible to a Core Twenty One that changed my life forever.

Even though I owned an art gallery in New York and was the Director of the Photography Program at Parsons School for Design, working in Russia was beyond all of my life experience. I did not know the language so could not communicate or read the signage and did not have any real knowledge of the culture or what the people were like. Nor did I know what to expect in terms of accommodations or food, how to get around, how business was done, what the local customs were, or how I would create an opportunity for myself to give the much desired lecture or curate an exhibition. Quite honestly, I didn't even know if those opportunities existed. The *Walls of My Knowledge* were firmly built in the American and European experiences that I had to that point. Despite doing some research before traveling all my assumptions were incorrect and I learned as I went.

I was living far beyond my boundaries. Doing so taught me to take greater risks and trust my instincts in other parts of my life, as well as how to make better choices and see the world and my place in it in an entirely different way. I learned that I had far greater control over my life than imagined and that the opportunities in it were vast. More often than not I was the limiting factor, not the outside forces that I believed were holding me back. I finally understood that when facing something unexpected I just had to take the first step and move the *Walls of My Knowledge* out a little farther.

Thinking and living outside the *Walls of Your Knowledge* is certainly not limited to art and travel. Throughout this chapter you will find examples of people doing so in a number of fields. It is easy to believe that the moments when people move beyond the *Walls of Their Knowledge* are rare, but it is far more common than you might imagine.

Fashion designer and creative director Reed Krakoff's first job after college was as an illustrator at Ralph Lauren. Ralph was a great place for a young designer to land as the company was a powerhouse. Reed learned a lot during his time at Ralph Lauren, but after four years it was time to make a change. A few years earlier Tommy Hilfiger had launched his now iconic brand. The company was not large, but the advertising was provocative and the clothing was getting a lot of attention. When Tommy offered Reed a job as the Head of Design he said yes. It was a substantial and satisfying step forward that redefined his *Who Can I Be* and expanded the *Walls of His Knowledge*.

It was an interesting moment in fashion: hip-hop was coming to the fore and well-known brands were being bought by larger conglomerates. During this period, Gucci hired Tom Ford, who pioneered the position of Creative Director. A Creative Director is a Head of Design who is also part of the company's executive suite, taking part in decisions regarding the business side of the brand as well as overseeing designing the clothes. Traditionally the business and creative sides of the company were separate but as we learned in Chapter Four, by utilizing the Agile Process, being flexible, and incorporating a range of informed perspectives into the decision-making process, you increase the chance for a positive outcome.

After Gucci's success other brands incorporated Creative Directors into their business teams and Tommy asked Reed to take on the new role. Reed said yes but he had to learn on the job and was pushed beyond the *Walls of His Knowledge* daily. He tells the story of being on his first photoshoot, "I had never been on a set before and I was working with a very serious photographer and kept getting in the way. I didn't know what I was doing for the first six months. But it was really funny, I'd never done it before." There wasn't anyone to call or any place to learn more about the position as the job was new to the industry, but Reed was good at what he did and learned from each experience. For the next five years he ran the front end of the business including some marketing, stores, and fashion design, while participating on the business side of the brand as well. During his time at Tommy the company grew from one hundred million dollars to a billion dollar company. Tommy Hilfiger was on its way to becoming an iconic brand central to 1990s rap and hip-hop, and Reed had gained a lifetime's worth of experience, expanding the *Walls of His Knowledge* while pushing himself personally and professionally along the way. This would continue to be the case throughout his career.

Every young business has to find the balance between a more traditional structure and the need to evolve to stay fresh and relevant. It is important for the company to stay focused on their mission, be fiscally responsible, not overextend themselves across too many products, or make management decisions that could harm the brand. On the other hand, it would be easy to play it too conservatively, ultimately losing momentum and missing opportunities.

The same concept applies to your life. You want to evolve and avoid stagnation, keeping life interesting and fresh and providing new opportunities along the way. New and ever-changing Summers should be part of your way of thinking. Work to move beyond the *Walls of Your Knowledge* and *Make Me Comfortable* to give yourself new opportunities to learn and grow as you assess *Who Am I*, *Who Can I Be*, and *Yes, But Who Am I Really*. Fulfilling the desire for change can be as simple as learning the piano or as big as changing your relationship, leaving your job, or moving to another city. Whatever you decide, remember that refreshing your life means taking calculated risks, ones that stretch you and the people around you. Change can, and at times will, be dramatic, but it doesn't mean that you have to blow up your life. Like a new business, find the line between the things that are working in your life and those you want to change. Let yourself evolve, stay fresh, and relevant, as you take the steps necessary to achieve your Twenty One. Try to not overextend yourself across too many projects, but keep moving forward, experimenting, and breaking down the *Walls of Your Knowledge* as you go.

When in New York, I co-taught a course called Projected Environments. In the class, students learned how to create immersive environments utilizing projection and installations. My favorite assignment was to ask students to work in teams to create a projected environment without using any flat or solid surfaces. They could not project still images or video onto the ceiling, walls, screens, scrims, or any other physical object. Each group had four weeks to come up with a concept and present the completed project to the class.

The presentations were truly satisfying as teams came up with solutions that I never would have imagined. For instance, one group used dry ice and projected on the smoke it gave off as it ran through troughs and holes in the walls of the box they had constructed. Another group set up a projector in a dark room and gave everyone spray bottles. When you sprayed mist through the air an image appeared. What you saw changed depending on where you stood in relation to the projector. When five or six people sprayed water together, an ever-changing series of colors and shapes appeared across the room bringing the entire piece to life. It was a magical little moment that the students loved.

The purpose of the assignment was to get students to think outside of their comfort zone personally, creatively, and intellectually. We watched them grow as they came up with an answer to a problem they did not think had a solution. By removing the problem solving processes they typically relied on, we were able to move them beyond the *Walls of Their Knowledge* and away from *Make Me Comfortable*, opening the door to new ways of thinking. Through this simple assignment students learned that they could do more than they had imagined, gaining confidence in their creativity and problem solving ability while learning something new.

We are comfortable asking artists and others to come up with new ways of making and thinking but we often struggle when we ask ourselves to do the same. It is easier to hold others to a higher standard, particularly when it comes to innovation, as our Blind Spots keep us from believing that we have the ability to think in new and imaginative ways.

Some people reading this may say that they are not creative or innovative so of course they don't think beyond their personal, social, and cultural knowledge boundaries, but we are not simply talking about art here. We are talking about life and your way of perceiving the world and your place in it. As you have seen with Kodo, Katya, Elinor, Cira, Pasang, and others, large changes in life begin with one decision, one step that takes you down the road toward fulfilling your Twenty One Summers. It may take time to achieve what you desire, but that is OK. The process is already in place, you just need to begin.

Perception is central to your ability to achieve and appreciate your Twenty One. There are times when life can be filled with negative thoughts about yourself, your situation, and others, making change seem unachievable. These thoughts consume your time and energy. They can immobilize you, keeping you from taking the first step toward positive change or moving forward with plans already in progress. If you are not careful, you can become stuck in this cycle with negative thoughts and excuses becoming your self-image and the way others view you as well. You may initially get attention when talking about how hard life is or what is going wrong in your life, but over time that attention diminishes along with your ability to develop a healthy perspective. The Blind Spots *Who Am I* and *Yes, But Who Am I Really* can come into play as you begin question your self-identity and strive to define yourself in a positive context.

If you find yourself in one of these cycles, stop, check yourself, take a breath, and refocus your energy on the positive changes you want to make, the things that you aspire to as opposed to the people or things that bring you down. Take a few minutes each day and remind yourself of the potential that exists in your life. If it helps, make your list a mantra that you repeat every morning. Imagine the changes that you would like to see occur and the next step that you can take to achieve your dreams and desires. Each small change for the better will help you break free from cycles of negative thinking and those who manifest them. This alone will become its own force for change, making you happier and more self-empowered.

As we mentioned in Chapter Two, educators, family, friends, communities, and societies often tell us that we cannot or should not grow or succeed. When you question your ability to change you may be defining yourself based on other people's ways of living while limiting your possibilities. The same thing occurs when you feel that you must live safely within the *Walls of Your Knowledge*. You hold yourself back based on the limitations of your knowledge and experience or perhaps the opinions of people around you and community that you live in. Take a moment and look at your *Who Am I, Who Am I Supposed To Be, Make Me Comfortable*, and *Who Can I Be*, and see how they may be keeping you inside the *Walls of Your Knowledge*. Step outside of the way you view the world and allow yourself to come up with new ideas for your Twenty One and the rest of your life. It can be hard to trust yourself or change your way of thinking, but if you begin to take those first often tenuous steps you will be happy with the outcome.

Derrick's experience in tech offers examples of people who have not only moved beyond the *Walls of Their*

Knowledge but those of society as well. There are a handful of inventions that represent truly innovative moments of genius and other innovations that are the product of good timing, smart choices, and existing technology. The latter shows the fallacy of the myth of genius, which is the belief that you must be a genius to create something extraordinary. The truth is all of us can do wonderful things if we begin to look at the world around us differently.

Google falls into the first category. The founders of Google were three Stanford students: Larry Page, Sergey Brin, and the less well-known Scott Hassan who left Google once Larry and Sergey decided to form a company. Don't feel bad for Scott, he invested in Google in the beginning so he's doing fine. Google created PageRank, a way of searching the web based on data from each individual page, something previous search engines could not do. In addition to being quick and efficient Google's technology is able to grow as the internet does, thereby giving its users quick access to extraordinary amounts of information. In doing so, it has changed the way we search and learn online. If those three students hadn't thought outside the *Walls of Their Knowledge* running a search online would be quite different. This way of operating is now being challenged by AI as information is once again being aggregated in a new way. The need to stay nimble and evolve is ever present.

On a side note, though search has been in place for decades, it might surprise you to know that almost half of all searches conducted today are brand new and have never been seen by the app before. We have a wonderfully insatiable appetite to learn and grow as we strive to move the *Walls of Our Knowledge* out farther and evolve as individuals and a society.

Uber, DoorDash, and Airbnb are examples of innovations that are the result of good timing and smart choices. The founders of these companies saw an opportunity to use existing technology to develop products that helped solve a problem in people's lives. They adjusted their vision when products failed or the environment changed and put in the time and hard work necessary to deliver a successful product. This last point is essential, as time and hard work are unavoidable aspects of success.

Garret Camp founded Uber based on a very simple idea that made our lives easier. He asked himself what would happen if you could request a ride on your phone instead of waiting for a cab or trying to get a car in a small town or rural area. Garret is a great innovator. He took advantage of GPS and payment systems that were new to mobile devices, but the creation of Uber was not like Google's PageRank search. As it turns out, almost any of us could have created Uber. We didn't, but Camp did as he allowed himself to think past the *Walls of His Knowledge* in a way that the rest of us did not and brought his idea to life.

Airbnb is another example of an idea that had great timing, hard work, and the perfect mix of technology on its side. The initial goal of Airbnb was to make money during tech conferences in San Francisco when hotels were booked and prices high. Founders Brian Chesky, Joe Gebbia, and Nathan Blecharczyk launched a website called Air Bed and Breakfast and offered air mattresses to their guests, which is where the "Air" in Airbnb came from. It took a while for Airbnb to catch on, but they are now an important player in travel. As with Uber timing was important, Airbnb would not have been possible without online payments and other technology that had become commonplace on smartphones.

The last and one of my favorite examples is Pinterest, founded by Ben Silbermann. A native Iowan, Ben moved to Silicon Valley in the early 2000s where he found work in the customer service department at Google answering customers questions. Ben wanted to do more than to work in customer service and talked regularly about his desire to create his own business. He wasn't going to make that happen while working at Google, so his girlfriend finally told him to stop talking and start his own company. In 2008, he did. His first idea was a mobile shopping app that competed with Amazon, a daunting task, it was not a success. However, at the core of his app there was a great idea that would one day become Pinterest.

Ben was an avid collector and thought that the idea of collecting things could be successful as a stand alone application, so he collaborated with designer Evan Sharp to create Pinterest. The idea was pretty simple, people could collect and "pin" photographs to their page and share them with others on social media. Created in 2010, Pinterest was pre-TikTok, pre-Instagram, and Facebook was just gaining ground, so the space to collect and share photographs was wide open. Still, Pinterest struggled to gain acceptance and Ben traveled across the country to everything from knitting conferences to larger conventions to promote his product. The first widespread use of the Pinterest occurred in Des Moines, Iowa, which Ben attributes to his mother telling people in town to use the app. Momentum built slowly, but in 2012, Pinterest finally took off as social media became popular. The company is now worth twenty five billion dollars and continues to grow. Ben's story is a great example of someone who had a desire to change his life and decided to take action instead of simply talking about his dreams and aspirations. He initially failed, but collected feedback, adjusted his goals, and then through hard work, determination, and thinking beyond the *Walls of His and Society's Knowledge*, succeeded.

You need to do the same, there are existing skill sets and potential opportunities in your life that you can use as stepping stones toward your larger goals. You don't need to come up with an entirely new invention or way of doing things, but you do need to look at opportunities and challenges in a different way. Find something in your life that you would like to improve or change. Then look for potential solutions or pathways to make that change happen. Imagine obstacles as things to overcome or as guideposts telling you when and where you need to adjust your goals and find the opportunities hiding just behind them.

In the same way Ben found Pinterest inside his failed shopping app, you can find success in your challenges and failures. Look for synergies and relationships between things that may not at first seem obvious, you will be surprised at the opportunities that you may find there. Like Garret Camp building Uber or the guys who started Airbnb, sometimes you need to look at the tools and potential opportunities that the world is presenting and then decide how you can bring them together to create something new in your life.

Some people refuse to believe that there are new opportunities available to them, falling into a habit of self-defeat as they consciously or subconsciously undermine themselves when things are going well. They think that it is better to end a good thing as opposed to experiencing what they believe is inevitable hurt or disappointment. Deep down they hold on to the idea that something bad will always happen, projecting multiple Blind Spots onto every situation.

Consistently negative thoughts and beliefs will remove opportunities and limit your ability to see the world in new ways. A negative point of view will draw in the *Walls of Your Knowledge*, creating a very small space in which to live. If you feel the walls closing in it is a sign that you need to examine your goals, adjust your way of thinking, and work harder than ever to create positive change.

Stop reading for a moment and make sure that this dynamic is not at work in your life. Consider how you view life, love, success, and happiness: do negative thoughts or inevitable failure come to mind when you think about any of these topics? If the answer is yes, then take a deep breath and focus on the positive changes you want to make in your life. Begin the step-by-step process of changing your perspective and disempowering the negative self-defeating narrative that you have running inside of your head. Becoming aware of your thought process is the first step. Once you are aware of a negative dialog at work in your life, look for how and when it occurs in your daily routine. Do these thoughts occur at a certain time of day? Are they connected with a specific person, place, or action? If you find yourself triggered or making a choice that will create problems, stop, slow down, and reconsider your decision. Let your mind clear and make yourself wait a beat before moving forward. If you catch yourself thinking that something bad is inevitably going to happen, remind yourself that this is a perception, not a reality. It is a perspective that you have learned somewhere and internalized, a habitual dialog that needs to change.

During these moments, focus on the next step that you need to take to achieve a positive outcome. Allow yourself a small success, one that is proof of your control over a negative narrative. This may be reading a chapter in a book, having a smaller serving at your next meal, cleaning a closet or drawer, giving yourself time to review your goals, or listening to a podcast or audiobook. Then work to repeat these steps, making them a habit that you don't allow yourself to break. Begin to connect these new actions to something familiar so they become part of your routine. Maybe you do ten push-ups before you make coffee in the morning. Keep it simple. The small steps you take will lead to larger successes and ultimately to changing your life or empowering someone else's. Expanding the *Walls of Your Knowledge* and removing self-defeating narratives is an ongoing process. Be aware, as a deeply learned narrative can pop up anytime, anywhere, even when things are going well.

Failure and disappointment are unavoidable and we do not get everything we want or need, but that is very different from defeating yourself or allowing yourself to be defeated. It takes time to believe that you will ultimately be successful in your endeavors. Just keep your momentum moving forward and find the pathway, your pathway, to your goals. Keep adjusting your Twenty One and the way that you are working to achieve them. One day you will be surprised at how far you have come. Never forget that you are a rare and valuable individual who deserves to have good happen in their life. Hold on to that thought. Remove the negative dialogs, whether they are in your mind or coming from others. Start valuing and trusting yourself. Be strong. It will change everything.

Like Ben Silbermann or Katya, work to apply your skills in a way that is timely and makes sense for where you are in your life. Doing so will give you a better chance for success. Your choices after graduation will be different than those mid-career, as an empty nester, or at retirement. Be flexible, don't hold on to your plans too tightly as you will only frustrate yourself. Adjust to changes in your life and the inevitable obstacles and opportunities that come along the path to your Twenty One. Overcoming the challenges you face along the way will only make your success sweeter.

As you take risks and life evolves, there will inevitably be moments of failure or times when things do not go as planned. Not all failure is a bad thing. Embrace positive forms of failure as they can be wonderful learning experiences. Think of positive failure as taking a risk or trying something new, but not getting it quite right. As we saw in Chapter Three, these are Moments of Learning, opportunities to expand the *Walls of Your Knowledge* through new experiences, research, and applying the Iterative and Agile Processes. Another place where failure should be embraced is when working through an iterative problem solving process. You want to discover the flaws in a new product, artwork, or process, incorporating what you learn as you go. Doing so will increase your chance for success. Positive forms of failure will be part of learning any new skill such as playing an instrument, painting, sports, coding, or learning a new language. Some struggle is inevitable as you explore new experiences and try new things, but as long as you are working hard, staying focused, doing your research, and putting in the time, these forms of failure are absolutely acceptable as they are part of the process.

Negative forms of failure come from not being prepared, procrastination, a lack of communication, not putting in the necessary work, creating a toxic environment, or not paying attention to detail. These are the types of failure that you want to avoid as it means that you are consciously or unconsciously undermining yourself and your ability to succeed. It may also be a sign that you are not willing to accept or embrace success. Another way to look at this is that positive forms of failure ultimately lead to expanding the *Walls of Your Knowledge*, while negative forms of failure shrink them.

This leads us to the final point, stay focused and put in the work that it takes to create positive change. As you have seen throughout the book, you have the power and ability to effect change in your life. Failure can be defeating for some people but for others it is the catalyst for success. Don't let failure define you, learn from it and come back stronger and smarter than before. A quote that I heard once comes to mind: "How do I respond to failure? The same way that I respond to success, by working harder."

Andrew Hawken calls himself part of England's 11 Plus generation. While he was in primary school, a standardized problem solving exam was given to all eleven year olds during their last year of class. The test was supposed to match students to the appropriate school for their skill set and future career. Students who passed would have access to grammar schools and were on the path to becoming lawyers, solicitors, and so on. Those who did not were sent to technical schools to prepare them to be manual laborers.

Andrew will tell you that failing the 11 Plus test was a key moment in his life, one that became an important part of his personality. It gave him the drive and desire to create a career that denied the results of that exam and proved the test and those who administered it wrong. The pathway to that career wasn't easy and it certainly wasn't logical, but it was beautiful.

After the exam Andrew ended up in a technical school in the West Midlands. He didn't think that he was good at anything and didn't have any idea what he wanted to be. The test just seemed to prove that point. While in English class his instructor saw a passion in him. He took Andrew aside and told him that he was one of the best English students he had taught at the school and gave him Ernest Hemingway's *A Farewell to Arms* to read. At this point Andrew had to make a choice: he could either embrace his belief that he was not good at anything and accept his pathway, or he could trust the faith that his instructor had in him and read the novel. Says Andrew, "It was like an explosion went off in my head. I couldn't believe this book and how wrapped up I was in it. I just became obsessed and began to read other literature. Suddenly I began to think, OK, I can do something." That was the beginning, a small step, a book introduced into a world of insecurity and disbelief. Then another book, each one helping Andrew believe in himself a little more. The *Walls of Andrew's Knowledge* had been blown apart. He began to hunger for more and started to look for opportunities where he could put his new knowledge and desire to work. His teacher had just opened the door to a Core Twenty One.

For you, the first step may be baking your first loaf of bread, fixing or renovating your first car, doing one pull-up, or writing the first line of a novel. With each step your belief in yourself will become stronger and after time a pathway will open that wasn't there before. As you repeat the process your ability to redefine who you are will grow as well. You will begin to think beyond your boundaries and see new opportunities for yourself that did not exist a short time ago. If you are lucky you will find a *Teacher* or *Mentor* like Andrew did. If not, you certainly have the power to take that first step yourself. It is your life, begin the process of making it what you want it to be.

For Andrew's sixtieth birthday his close friend Daglar gave him a first edition of *A Farewell to Arms* to commemorate his hard work, success, and the path that he took from failing the 11 Plus to his current career. His interest in literature got him into a university; he was the first in his family to do so. Once there, Andrew was hardly a standout student but his love for reading and writing did not disappear. Still unsure of what he wanted to do he went to the local newspaper to see if they would allow him to intern just to get some experience. While he was there the phone rang. A local boy had fallen off some scaffolding and Bert, the editor, sent Andrew to find and interview him. Andrew knocked on hundreds of doors until he finally found the boy. When the boy's mother answered the door, she said, "Oh, Bert sent you." Bert had known where the boy was all along. Andrew got the interview and picture and then headed back to the newsroom. Andrew had proven how much he loved to write and how hard he was willing to work to achieve his goals and was hired. He spent his entire third year of college writing for the newspaper.

Just like the businesses mentioned earlier in the chapter, timing, hard work, and technology have all played a large role in Andrew's career. Working at the local newspaper, he found himself in one of the last places where typewriters were being used. When computers were introduced, the newspaper's union went on strike to keep them out of the newsroom as they would be taking jobs away from union members. At that point Andrew realized that life was not always going to be the same at the little paper he loved. Change was inevitable and if he did not change as well he was going to be left behind once again. Andrew was one of a few who embraced change instead of holding onto the past to his own detriment. He left the newspaper and found a position with the British Broadcasting Corporation (BBC) a much larger and more progressive news corporation with a national and international footprint. This was the next big step in his evolution and hardly the last.

A lot of people express anger or frustration over unexpected changes like the one Andrew faced. You have a choice in these situations: you can either learn, evolve, and stay ahead of the change, or quite possibly find yourself and your opportunities diminished because you wanted to *Make Yourself Comfortable* and were not open to redefining *Who Can I Be*. It can be more comfortable to stay within the *Walls of Your Knowledge* than to learn a new skill set and take on the challenge of changing your life like Andrew and Reed did, but taking on those challenges and growing past your Blind Spots is a large part of what your Twenty One is about.

The technological changes that Andrew's union fought in the newsroom have transformed the way we think, live, and learn. Our ability to learn collectively has accelerated as ChatGPT, Google, YouTube, and other platforms provide access to information unavailable in the same manner prior to their launch. Individuals can now learn skills that had only been available by traveling to a school, university, conference, apprenticeship, workshop, thinktank, or leading corporation. You are no longer stuck in a small town or remote region without a gateway to experts and global communities. If you can learn how to use these programs to access *Teachers, Mentors,* and information seamlessly, the potential is enormous. The key is to find information from credible sources, people, and organizations with real experience in the area that you are interested in.

Given the knowledge and connectivity at our fingertips we have the potential to achieve our Twenty One Summers much more quickly. I can learn French with an instructor in Paris three times a week and study on an app with ease and efficiency. Collective learning is now ubiquitous. Access has increased as barriers to entry have disappeared. This, along with the rise of work at home and digital nomads has made it increasingly comfortable to take on projects and lifestyle changes that would have been much harder, if not impossible, just a short time ago. We enjoy a historically unequaled opportunity to create, ability to collaborate, and access to education that provides an extraordinary sense of freedom if you embrace and utilize the opportunity.

We have experienced a massive shift in terms of access to information and what is possible in our lives. However, many of us do not explore the wealth of knowledge that is available to us, even the most technologically savvy are not always taking full advantage. Quite honestly, many of us are living in the same manner that people have for hundreds of years, though with laptops, iPads, and smartphones.

Roughly 12,000 years ago, humans began to settle down to farm which led to the end of roaming for many tribal groups. Communities began to spring up and villages, towns, and cities took on an increasingly important role in people's lives. At the time there were multiple barriers to someone's ability to grow and change, one of which was an often singular perspective in the local community. The *Walls of an Individual's Knowledge* were founded on local culture and the experience of those around them. As we have learned, this creates strong high walls and a small space for our knowledge. In these situations, decision-making is deeply influenced by family, friends, colleagues, and community expectations and standards, which often leads to limited personal, career, and lifestyle choices.

As individuals we are positioned to exponentially expand the *Walls of Our Knowledge* and in doing so change our lives. So, why do we often view our lives in the same manner as people who lived in a small town or village hundreds of years ago? Allowing our choices to be limited by local expectations while holding on to the past like the newsroom trying to keep typewriters.

The key to moving past that perspective is to look at your life free from the constraints that you and your community have put into place. If it is true that our ability to acquire new knowledge, learn new skills, and travel around the world exists in ways that were not possible just a short time ago, then why aren't you regularly moving the *Walls of Your Knowledge* outward and looking beyond those boundaries into endless possibilities? At the least you should be asking yourself new questions and taking advantage of the information and technology at your disposal. What Blind Spots are holding you back?

For many, expanding the *Walls of Their Knowledge* is driven by curiosity and the desire to learn. This doesn't begin with attending school or getting a degree, it is an innate or cultivated desire to grow, to consume knowledge, life, and experience, a way to constantly expand the *Walls of Your Knowledge* as your life evolves and you strive to fulfill your Twenty One Summers. We all know people who never seem to stop moving forward in life, amazing fashion designers, artists, readers, supporters of the arts, coders, cooks, knitters, photographers, mechanics, writers, musicians, athletes, anime enthusiasts, gamers, travelers, collectors, entrepreneurs, and so many more. Learning is an essential part of their and your Twenty One Summers; it will expand the *Walls of Your Knowledge*, help you understand the opportunities life presents, and move you past *Make Me Comfortable*. It will also inform *Yes, But Who Am I Really*, as well as *Who Am I, Who Am I Supposed To Be*, and *Who Can I Be*.

You might say that you've never been good at learning, but by learning we don't just mean in school. You may not like research or were never good in class, but the fact is you can't make a loaf of bread without reading the recipe, use a new phone without at least knowing the basics, or play pickleball without understanding the court and rules. There are many ways to learn that will move you along the pathway to your Twenty One. Embrace them, there is truly something for everyone.

Whenever I have worked with someone at the top of their field I have consistently found them to be curious and engaged with a broad range of subjects. They consume life, experiences, and information, combining them to design a life and career that they enjoy. Reed Krakoff is a perfect example of this, someone who by nature aspires to create a richly informed and satisfying lifestyle. I met Reed while working with him as a photography consultant when he was the Creative Director for COACH. He is without question one of the most talented, curious, and well referenced people I have ever met. His drive to learn and experience new things is boundless, which is one of the great pleasures of working with him.

Reed moved to COACH after leaving Tommy Hilfiger. The company was looking for a change and at thirty six years old he became their first Creative Director overseeing the entire creative side of the business along with participating in the business side and their new global initiatives. Though he had held the same title at Tommy, the first year at COACH was an education in what it was like to work for a big publicly owned company. His management skills and talent as a designer helped facilitate a successful transition.

As Reed noted in our interview, "When I started a lot people were surprised. I was so young. There were people at the company who were against the big changes. It always takes more in terms of time and money than imagined, but reinventing a brand is like renovating a house. It takes twice as long as you thought and it's always hard. It takes a lot of guts. You have to take a chance and be willing to face the consequences. That's one of the reasons it doesn't happen at many companies. It can be painful." Like Tommy, COACH became one of the brands of the moment. Reed described the process, "It was the same thing, the brand just had so much momentum, but there was a cultural piece to this as well. It just fit. Everything just started clicking, the marketing, the product, the stores, and the business was just on fire. For ten years it was growing every quarter." Though it is true that COACH fit the cultural and social trends of the moment, it is also true that Reed's understanding of culture, feel for the marketplace, and business savvy played a large role in the brand's success. When Reed left the COACH it had grown from a five hundred million to a five billion dollar company.

Reed's understanding of contemporary culture was not a surprise given his diverse interests. Over time I learned that he was one of the country's leading collectors of twentieth century and contemporary furniture and design, as well as a collector of painting, sculpture, and books on art and design. Reed and his wife share a passion for interior design and were in the midst of selecting and designing a new home, one of a handful they would go on to renovate as part of their creative collaboration. Reed consumed knowledge and culture as part of this process. His plate was full, but you never would have known it given his relaxed confidence, focus, and the pleasure he found in what he was doing.

As it often does, Reed's curiosity and interest in the arts has crossed over from his personal life into his work, influencing store design and touching fine art, fashion, and publishing, as each project created new opportunities that have impacted other parts of life. His ability to recognize style and value is a talent that has served him well as a creative, collector, and designer.

Every time we speak he is looking at new possibilities, and it becomes apparent how wide his boundaries are and how minimal his fear of failure. Though I was already open to taking chances and trying new things when we met, it was eye-opening to work with someone who consistently turned ideas into realities. As we spent more time together I began to embrace potential and possibilities in life that I either had not seen or ignored. There was an incredible freedom that came with the understanding that most anything can be manifested if you can put together the right team and the right situation. I quickly became aware of how often we hold ourselves back. We limit our options because we believe that we cannot, or should not, take a risk or open ourselves to a fresh perspective. *Who Am I, Who Am I Supposed To Be, Make Me Comfortable,* the *Walls of Our Knowledge,* and *Yes, But Who Am I Really* truly do keep us from trying new things and living a more fulfilling life.

Photography was an excellent example of Reed's perspective on life. Even though taking photographs was a rather new pursuit he dedicated himself to learning and quickly took on the challenge of photographing global campaigns and creating books. This ultimately manifested itself in campaigns for COACH and Tiffany as well as a number of books featuring his photographs. The first project we worked on was a cover and spread of Reed's then Hampton's home for Elle Décor Magazine, bringing together his interest in photography, contemporary design, the arts, homes, and interior design. Though he had explored photography, an architectural shoot for a well-respected publication was a big step forward. His focus while learning was impressive. There was a humility and open mindedness in his willingness to learn the technical and creative skills necessary to achieve his goals. He was driven to improve with each shoot and the evolution of his work exemplified that. He understood the need to listen respectfully to a diverse set of opinions and appreciated the value of learning from others, as well as from books and other resources. Reed describes it as follows, "You know, all of the things I am interested in kind of run into each other. And I like that kind of combination, bringing together of all those things and coming up with something unexpected in terms of what you create, what you design, what you study, or what you're interested in. There is always an interesting outcome." He went on to explain, "The books we made were a way to explore other interests. Honestly, I think it was a way to learn more about whatever the topic was, and to get to know the people behind it. The experience itself was super important, it was not just about the product that we made at the end."

As I have often said, each skill or opportunity that you have builds on another. Reed is right, oftentimes the experience itself is more important than the result. The people that you meet, the success and failure that you experience, expanding the *Walls of Your Knowledge*, challenging *Who Can I Be* and *Yes, But Who Am I Really*, understanding new possibilities, and the satisfaction of having tried something new are all invaluable.

About twelve years into his tenure at COACH, the company decided to launch a higher end line of shoes, hand bags, garments, and accessories under the Reed Krakoff name. It was an opportunity to bring together many of the things Reed loved and do them at a more elevated level.

When COACH later made the decision to spin the new company off, Reed and a group of investors decided to take it private. During its run the team at Reed Krakoff did some incredible things including dressing Michelle Obama for her Vogue magazine cover, winning the Accessories Award from the Council of Fashion Designers of America, and producing some wonderful shows. Within the first three years, the company had grown to around thirty million dollars in sales, which is an enormous amount of luxury in a short period of time, but competing financially with Prada, Gucci, and Fendi, companies that were part of multi-million dollar conglomerates, was difficult. The business was not sustainable as a stand alone company so they paid all of the employees and Reed closed the brand. It was a difficult choice to make, but the right one.

Moving on from a company that you helped grow and another that you started from scratch takes time. You need to process what you have learned, change perspective, and recalibrate your Twenty One. As we have seen many times some of the best transitions happen at the most challenging moments in life, for Reed that moment led to Tiffany & Co.

Working as the Creative Director at Tiffany was a dream job, one that allowed Reed to combine his professional skill set and personal interests. He and his team did some wonderful things at the tradition filled company. One of the most visible was collaborating with Lady Gaga as she wore the original 128.54-carat yellow diamond Tiffany Diamond on the red carpet the year that she won an Oscar for her role in *A Star Is Born*. Reed also launched the Blue Box Café with the extraordinary chef Daniel Boulud and created a concept around home called Everyday Objects. Each project was a marriage of Reed's interests personally, creatively, and professionally, as well as his desire to push the envelope as he had done at each stop in his career.

Reed is now part of a group that invests in fashion brands and helps them develop their business. When we last spoke, he had started making ceramics and was considering the subject for his next photobook. As usual, one project was linked to another with each step building on the success of other endeavors.

You may say that you have little in common with someone in the fashion industry, but Reed's story contains numerous themes from throughout the book that apply to your life as well. Each experience, each skill learned, each success or failure, has led to new opportunities. The same can be true for you. You don't need to start with something big, small accomplishments build confidence and credibility that can be applied to larger goals. Each step you take will expand the *Walls of Your Knowledge*, opening the pathway toward your Twenty One.

Look for ways to incorporate the things you love into other parts of your life and let them inform your Twenty One as well. Since leaving Microsoft Derrick has brought together many of the things he loves. He has designed a new life that includes photography, sports, travel, and consulting. It has been a rich and satisfying combination. My desire to live a life that allows me to travel, create, and consult, has taken years to build, but the result has been well worth the effort. Reed's willingness to take risks and go down a pathway that led to groundbreaking positions at each stop in his career is inspiring. The Agile and Iterative Processes were evident as he developed new products and ideas, evolving as a designer and businessperson while responding to input from customers, creatives, the marketplace, contemporary culture, and the executive suite. This became one of his hallmarks, as did a willingness to learn, take risks and explore.

As I sat in my apartment in Madison that morning after graduation, I didn't understand the possibilities that existed or how my lifestyle and career choices were limited by the community that I had grown up in, nor did Derrick as he bartended or coded for that long forgotten start-up. Expanding the *Walls of Our Knowledge* was going to be a lifelong pursuit, one that would lead to unexpected lifestyles and experiences. I couldn't have imagined working in casting in Los Angeles, being a fashion photographer, running a photography program at a university, owning an art gallery in New York, being part of State Department delegations in Russia, or writing this book. If Derrick had followed the advice of his family, friends, and local community, computer science would not have been his degree choice, and he would have missed out on a groundbreaking career creating products that have changed the way we all live.

The communities we grew up in were wonderful places, but they held on to ways of thinking that could have inhibited our lives. We each looked beyond the *Walls of Our Knowledge* and found new opportunities that were not only exciting but changed the trajectory of our personal lives and careers. With each step we began to believe in our futures and open our minds to possibilities we could not have imagined years before. I certainly couldn't have envisioned the way my life has turned out when putting together the first version of my Twenty One Summers after college. That is the beauty of identifying the Blind Spots at work in your life, doing so expands your vision and moves you past the barriers holding you back.

Defining and embracing a clear set of goals is a powerful process. Ultimately it provides you with new pathways through life and the chance to feel fulfilled. Doing so will help you value the time that you have and the things that you love. Believe in the life you want to live and strive to become the person you want to be. Do not let the *Walls of Your Knowledge* become a barrier to your ability to grow and change. Keep an open mind, embrace your interests, and let them inform your possibilities. Live your life to the fullest. You only have so many summers to do so and, as you know, time passes all too quickly.

Chapter Six
The Trade

New York was always intimidating to me. Growing up in the Midwest, New York seemed large and ominous, daunting at best, dangerous and unforgiving at worst. Leaving the comfort and familiarity of Wisconsin and moving to Los Angeles was a challenge as the culture and lifestyle were unlike anything I had experienced before. Going to New York was an entirely different proposition. New York was demanding personally, physically, and professionally. When you move there you take on the city as well as life, all while competing against the best in the world. From the moment I arrived it felt as if my Twenty One were almost within my grasp, all I needed to do was make them happen. That was not going to be as easy as I imagined. I've never worked so hard in so many ways. Yet in the end the city would become one of my greatest loves and allies, and a pathway to countless new Summers.

We have talked at length about the Blind Spots that hold us all back without us knowing it and the challenges we face as we work to move past them on the pathway to our Twenty One. There is celebration to be had as we achieve each success and there are also *Trades* that accompany them. With every decision we make we leave behind one set of options while opening the door to new possibilities. When I left Wisconsin to drive to Los Angeles I was leaving behind the safety and comfort of family, friends, and a life that I knew and understood. It was a *Trade* that I had to make if I wanted to have new experiences and explore the dream of working in the film industry. As mentioned earlier, it did not turn out as I thought, as both the industry and Los Angeles were not what that boy from the Midwest had imagined. Selling popcorn in a movie theater is hardly what college dreams are made of. That could have been a moment of crisis, but it became one of motivation. I had to find a new path through the city and my life, and to reimagine my Twenty One Summers as those I had on my list no longer belonged.

I visited Wisconsin regularly while away and it was wonderful to see everyone, but during one trip back I noticed that my parents were slightly different, as were many of my friends. My hometown was the familiar place that it always was, but it wasn't mine in the same way anymore. Lives had changed, people had aged, and our life experience and goals had diverged. Time passed and each trip home made it increasingly apparent that I was no longer the person that left. That is one of the *Trades* you can't really imagine. You can never predict how life will evolve when you are not around. I deeply respect the friends who stayed, built families, and supported the local community. It is a beautiful life for many, not for all. It just could never be mine.

Leaving a location or not living a lifestyle doesn't mean that you disrespect it. This isn't a competition and there isn't a hierarchy to the decision to stay or not with one being better than the other; it is about finding what is right for you.

Derrick was far more grounded in this area than me. Throughout his time in college, he traveled abroad to earn money for college. This sounds like a perfect way for a student to travel and earn, and it was, but there were *Trades* to be made as well. There always are. The summer after his first year in college he headed to Munich for a job that would pay for his next year's tuition and living expenses. Upon arriving, he pitched a tent in a local campground and saved all that he earned for school. It was hard work, but he had a summer to explore Germany and meet travelers from around the world. What he hadn't planned on was his girlfriend's reaction when he told her he was leaving Dublin for Germany. In Derrick's mind the relationship wasn't very serious and would easily survive the summer. His girlfriend felt quite the opposite and told him that if he left they would have to end their relationship. Traveling and earning for school was a great experience, and in retrospect the right choice, but the *Trade* was a painful one as it cost him his relationship. It was a lesson well learned, as we mentioned in Chapter Two, he and his partner Debbie traveled together for three months in Mexico, a *Trade* that led to Microsoft and a long lasting marriage.

At times, Derrick and I have both wondered what drives us to continually take on the challenges and opportunities that arise during life. The answer is always the same. There is an inescapable feeling inside, an unease that is at times indescribable and other times sharp, present. Its message is unavoidable: that a life change needs to happen or is about to occur. We also have a deep-seated desire to learn and grow, to see what the world has to offer in the short time we have here. A hunger to experience life fully before we are not able to, and with each new adventure, career choice, lifestyle choice, there have come new unimagined opportunities that have drawn each of us forward.

Ultimately there is an upside and downside to every *Trade*; outcomes that you cannot envision when you make the decision. That is inevitable, and OK. It is, life. There is a tendency to imagine that the potential downside of a *Trade* may be large and the upside small. Part of good decision making is assessing the downside risk, that makes sense, but our imagination can run away and soon we are creating worst case scenarios when really the opposite is true. Every step you take is down a pathway, it isn't an end in and of itself. If you move to a new city and it doesn't work out you can move to a place that is a better fit. If a job or career choice doesn't turn out as imagined you have multiple options for learning and career change. There are apprenticeships in the trades for jobs that pay well and are in demand, or you can learn new skills online, take classes, and find *Teachers* and *Mentors* across the globe. Remember your *Stars* are always there and if you are at a moment in life where you feel alone, there are groups, communities, and individuals around to provide support.

We don't often reach out to others when we are feeling alone or challenged, but that is exactly when the people who care are willing to be there for you. As we mentioned earlier, they may not always be the people you expect. It may be someone at a new job, in a baking class, at the library, or perhaps an old friend or long lost family member. During these moments the support you receive will make the transition during and after a *Trade* easier. My first few months in Los Angeles and New York were difficult, there were lonely days but giving up was not an option and with the help of a few friends I survived. You will too, or you will adjust your Twenty One and move in a different direction. The ability to adjust and evolve is an important part of finding and achieving your goals.

Work/life balance is always a question that comes into play when discussing *Trades* in life. The work/life balance that you desire is connected to your Twenty One and the decisions that you make to reach them. There are some things like being a professional athlete or musician, CEO, leading tech engineer, or running your own business that require much more than forty hours a week of learning, hard work, and dedication to achieve. We may wish this was not the case, but along with talent necessary to be one of the best in your field you need to devote the time it takes to learn the processes, develop skills, understand the language, and forge a nuanced understanding in your area of interest. Work like this is a labor of love; these are not pursuits that you can work toward and become successful in simply because you "would like to." In addition to talent you must truly love and desire what you do if you are going to endure the demanding process necessary to reach the peak of your abilities or top of your field.

Imagine football/soccer players like Lionel Messi, Jude Bellingham, Aitana Bonmati, or Sophia Smith and how many hours they put in each day to be one the greatest players in the game. That is in addition to their talent and the mental and emotional strength it takes to compete. We understand and accept the time and effort they have spent to achieve success in the same manner we understand Yo-Yo Ma's dedication to the cello. People don't care if Mozart was a good cook, Martin Luther King was a good painter, Elon Musk can sew, or Serena Williams is a great surfer. We know and respect Mozart as a composer, Martin Luther

King as a civil rights leader and orator, Elon Musk as an entrepreneur, and Serena Williams as the greatest women's tennis player of all time. Did or does each of them have other skills? No doubt, but we do not judge them on the things that they are, or were, not good at. We appreciate the exceptional skill and dedication that they have or had for one or two things. Each touched the world by focusing on what they did best. You should do the same. Don't waste time mourning your lack of ability at something or let others make you feel bad about what you cannot do. Focus on the things that you do well and celebrate them. You may not be the best in the world, or even the best at your job, school, class, or team right now. That is OK. Keep working, take those small steps forward, have patience, and trust the process.

If we accept and understand the extraordinary *Trades* truly successful people make to achieve their Twenty One, why do so many of us find it so hard to make the *Trades* we need to make to get ahead? Why do so many people believe they do not need to put in the time to or make any sacrifices to achieve their goals? Not all of us can be Messi or Bonmati, no matter how many hours we spend playing soccer, nor can we be Jamie Dimon, the CEO of Chase National Bank. We can, however, become better versions of ourselves. In doing so we can improve our lives in ways that will help us achieve our own Twenty One or bring us to a point that we can make *Trades* never dreamed of before. Would I have loved to be a professional soccer player? Sure. Was I talented enough? No, but I have talent in other areas that I was able to develop while playing soccer.

I'm glad that I focused on the things that were important to me and not on the parts of my life that others believed equaled success. Many people have tried to define what success should look like in my life and what my work/life balance should be. If I had followed their definitions so many of my Twenty One never would have happened. Work hard and trust yourself. Revel in your talents and appreciate those of others.

Each of the goals you set and *Trades* you make help define your work/life balance. My father worked at a factory all day but made the time to attend almost every sporting event that I was in from the time that I was seven until twenty five. I always appreciated him being there, but truly didn't realize the effort it took for him to come after a long day of work until I was older. Many of those days he must have been exhausted. But for him, working hard to earn enough to give his family a good life and being a good husband and father were primary goals. They were his Core Twenty One. Along with smaller goals like his vegetable and flower gardens every summer. With a ninth grade education, he took the work he could as a young man and made the *Trades* in life necessary to achieve his version of Twenty One Summers. He didn't love working in the factory, that I knew, but I also knew that he enjoyed the people he worked with, the comradery, and was proud of his ability to run and repair the machines. It was not until after he retired and took a part-time job on a nearby farm that I learned he had wanted to own a farm since he was a young boy. After retirement he was finally able to enjoy part of his Twenty One that none of us ever knew about. Perhaps that is part of what retirement is for, to try the things you didn't when you had a world full of responsibilities, including the responsibility of a full-time job that you may or may not have loved. Why not be a farmer and live some of your dreams? Dreams don't end at a certain age, or at least they shouldn't, they are just waiting for the right time to be set free.

Dad made the *Trades* he felt necessary to achieve the things he believed in most. That is something that I will forever respect. He had his own version of work/life balance. My mother worked as a secretary at a local grade school so that she could have the same vacation days as my sister and me. She loved working, interacting with people, and being out in the community, but she chose her job so that she could be at home with us when we were little. She too made *Trades* to create a work/life balance that fit her Twenty One.

There isn't a single answer regarding what your work/life balance should be. There are many experts who will tell you what portion of your life should consist of work, play, or family, but if you want to be Messi or Yo-Yo Ma, then those percentages may not apply to you. For them, work and play may be synonymous. The same shift may be true if you have bills that are overwhelming or a family member who needs a greater portion of your time. In those instances, your work/life balance will adjust accordingly. In the end, the division of time and effort that comprises your work/life balance is entirely up to you. Strive to find a balance that is healthy and gives you the best chance to achieve your goals. Be sure that those around you understand the work/life balance you want or need in your life. Be fair to those who are part of your life and include them in conversations about your goals and the *Trades* you will need to make to reach them. Communication is key to healthy relationships and success in every part of your life.

There are many things that we can't be in life, but so many other things that we can. By focusing on the things that you are not good at, as opposed to your strengths, you reinforce the Blind Spots *Who Can I Be, Who Am I Supposed To Be, Who Am I Really* and *Make Me Comfortable*. They can become a drum beat in your head keeping you from moving forward. Educational institutions reinforce this idea, often leaving us feeling as if we are failures if we are not good at a range of topics. That is not true. We all have our strengths and weaknesses. Embrace the things that you enjoy and the places you find success. If necessary, adjust your work/life balance to allow you to focus on those skills and opportunities.

For some, making excuses and complaining seems to be what they do best. Not only is it an empty and unfulfilling pursuit, it can keep you stuck in the same place for a very long time. Complaints may be covering up your fears, a bad habit, or become a comfortable blanket under which you can hide, but in the end they will cost you happiness and opportunity. Whatever the reason, excuses and rationalizations are not serving you as well as you imagine.

When you hear negative messages in your mind or from others it is time to change the narrative in your life. Do not let that input keep you away from your goals and dreams. Take a breath, step away from negative ideas or influences, quiet your thoughts, and then take a positive step toward one of your Twenty One. Give yourself one small success, a bit of strength and confidence, and let it feel good. All it takes is one act to start changing the dialog, whether that is telling yourself the negative messaging is not true or taking a step toward achieving a goal. Trust in yourself as you repeat this process and slowly become more self-assured. Repetition is important as it takes time to learn new ways of thinking and reacting. Remember to enjoy each success big or small, not to compete with others, and to work toward the best version of your life that you can create. If you want to be the best dance teacher in your hometown, go for it. Maybe you want to be a deacon or usher at your church, learn how to swim, or help run a local children's sports league, these are all admirable aspirations. Find your Twenty One Summers, make them your own and then begin to take on Blind Spots and make the *Trades* necessary to reach your goals.

Many people check in with themselves daily, developing an attitude of problem solving instead of defeat, of appreciating the good in life instead of focusing on the negative. Doing so is a *Trade* that you make in terms of your time, focus, and attitude. You choose to enjoy the beauty of a walk, a perfectly made muffin, the sound of a friend's voice, or a beautiful photograph. Appreciating these little things can be one of life's greatest satisfactions. Getting to the point that you are able to do so may mean increasing your awareness and adjusting your perspective. Awareness, because it is easy to get caught up in the responsibilities of your daily life and forget to appreciate the little things that can transform your attitude and enrich your day. Perspective, because the way that you view your day and the things that happen to you changes everything. If you constantly view things negatively, make excuses, and believe that you do not have any power, then that will become your reality. If you view life as a series of small pleasures and challenges presenting opportunities for self-empowerment and growth, then that will become your reality. Deciding to adjust your attitude and perspective is a *Trade*, one that is non-negotiable.

Sometimes we refuse to make the simplest *Trades*, even if they will be beneficial. There is truly an absurdity to those decisions. One day a friend of Derrick's commented on his photographs and asked how he could create similar pictures. Derrick told him that it was easy, "You just need to get up before sunrise and position yourself and your subjects to take advantage of the morning light." His friend responded that getting up at sunrise, ninety minutes earlier than usual, was out of the question. One early morning stood between Derrick's friend and the photographs that he has always wanted to take, yet that simple *Trade* is not one that he was willing to make. If he was willing to get up at 6:30am to go to work every day, why wasn't he willing to get up at 5:00am one morning to do something for himself? One small step, one little change. If you can't bring yourself to take the first step, the rest of the path will forever stay closed.

When I moved to Los Angeles, my singular focus was to find a job in the film industry. I had left my home and friends to achieve that goal. As you know things did not work out as planned. That magnified the decision to leave the casting agency that I was working at to pursue another career. Doing so was an enormous personal and professional *Trade* and a complete realignment of my Twenty One. The phone call home to tell my parents that I was going to become a photographer is vividly etched into my mind. I could feel the disappointment on the other end of the line as I told them of my decision. My Mom and Dad had been relieved to hear that I had found a place in the film industry and loved listening to the stories that came along with the job. They were rightfully concerned about how I was going to support myself and pay the bills and I respected that.

One of my first clients, Carl, kept me in business for the first couple years, slowly teaching me what it really meant to be professional. Carl, like Derrick and I, chose to *Teach* and *Mentor* people who work hard and care. People who act professionally, respect others' time, have the desire to learn, and are willing to put in the time, energy, and go the extra mile to make things happen. Carl's faith gave me confidence and over time I began working with larger clients. Despite his support there were struggles and, in the end, building a career as a successful photographer meant making the *Trade* to go back to school at The Art Center College of Design in Pasadena to develop my skills.

Graduating from Art Center and making the commitment to fashion photography led to multiple trips to New York to see if there was any interest in my work. The response was encouraging but jobs were slow to come and I began questioning the time and financial *Trades* that I was making. That was when I met Carla, an editor at Condé Nast. For reasons I still do not understand, Carla became a *Mentor.* Each time we met she gave me a little more insight into what it would take to be successful in the industry. It was early in my career, but I realized it was time for the next *Trade* and a move to New York City. A lot of energy had gone into Los Angeles, it represented my first professional achievement and a wonderful relationship, but if the move was going to happen it was time to go. It was a big decision. Failure was definitely a possibility.

There was also the possibility of success. Nobody was going to give that to me, but I was ready to take the next series of steps toward my new Twenty One, overcoming a number of Blind Spots along the way. The first was *Make Me Comfortable* as life and work in Los Angeles was comfortable. *Who Can I Be* and *Who Am I, Who Am I Supposed To Be*, and *Yes, But Who Am I Really* were also in play. Moving to New York meant a redefinition of who I was in my personal life, career, and at home. I wondered if I was strong enough, talented enough, and willing to work hard enough to make that happen. Was this who I was supposed to be? Over time those questions would answer themselves. What I didn't realize were the *Trades* necessary to succeed and survive after arriving. Yet I adjusted personally, professionally, and in terms of my Twenty One. That is what you do, as life evolves so do you. It is impossible to imagine all of the challenges, opportunities, and changes that you will face when making a *Trade*. Ultimately you have to trust yourself and move forward. A little faith goes a long way. In the end, the *Trades* made were undeniable, as were the costs and benefits.

Derrick faced similar challenges. After graduation he decided to leave Dublin for London. As the move to London neared, he realized that this *Trade* was different. Saying "goodbye" to friends and family was not the same as "see you soon." Sharing everyday life evolved into phone calls, holidays, and occasional visits. His relationships with friends and family changed while he was away. That was a *Trade* that he did not expect. Fresh out of college he had three hundred dollars, a new degree, and the confidence of those rare moments when you feel like the world is out there just waiting for you. Despite the challenges it was the perfect time for a change.

Derrick's move from London to Seattle involved the biggest *Trade* of his life so far. At that point, he and his partner Debbie had a nice life together, their relationship was strong and she was running a thriving business as a personal trainer. The proximity to family was a plus as well. They were, in a word, comfortable. However, Derrick began to feel uneasy. Work had become repetitive, and he didn't see a lot of room to grow in their office. He knew that the important projects were being done in the company's headquarters and if he wanted his career to thrive he would have to either leave Microsoft or move to Seattle. The difference between a comfortable life in London and the potential of a better or quite possibly worse life in Seattle was huge. Debbie would need to close her business and would not be able to work in the US for one year and Derrick did not have guaranteed success in the new office. It seemed an all or nothing choice without a clear answer. The Blind Spots *Make Me Comfortable*, *Who Can I Be*, *Who Am I*, and *Who Am I Supposed To Be* were all in play as the *Trade* meant asking a lot of questions about who Derrick and Debbie were and who they could be in Seattle. Questions that were beyond the *Walls of Their Knowledge* until they lived in the city for a while. So they convinced themselves that moving to Seattle was temporary and kept their London apartment in case things didn't work out. The move turned out to be fantastic. Upon arriving they decided to get married which allowed Debbie to restart her business in the US, and Derrick's career thrived as his projects became more engaging.

Trades are part of all of our lives. Derrick and I both know actors and dancers who decided to move to another city for a new role or a chance to be part of a company. Each time making a *Trade* without the guarantee of success. A friend, Mike, had to move to Indiana for a new job while his family stayed in Wisconsin and his children finished school. They missed each other deeply, but the new job turned out to be a good one and the decision benefited his family. Another couple, Mike and Maura, have had to move a number of times throughout their marriage as careers evolved and jobs were lost or gained. Friends and acquaintances in the military have had to change locations regularly. Every situation presents its own form of a *Trade*, whether it is one of your own choosing or one that life chooses for you.

Some *Trades* will be easy for you, others will be challenging. Giving up part of your morning routine to exercise for twenty minutes will be an obvious choice for many, but if you are getting children ready for school or have a long drive through crosstown traffic to work, it will be a much more difficult *Trade* to make. Giving up a coffee every morning to save enough to buy a new pair of shoes, a birthday gift for your partner, or to go on your dream vacation, may be an easy *Trade* for you, but we all know people who would not give up their morning coffee for anything. There is a benefit and a cost to both of those choices. Either option may seem completely rational to the person making the decision.

There are large *Trades* in life as well. Leaving a marriage or relationship because things have changed between you, your love has faded, or your goals are now different from one another. Giving up a child for adoption or deciding to adopt or foster a child, walking away from a toxic job and making the choice to take care of yourself, or making a career change to take a chance on a job you love, these are all substantial decisions. Remember Ben Silbermann, the founder of Pinterest who had to leave his job in customer service at Google to take on the dream of developing his own app? He traded job security for an opportunity to develop and launch a shopping app, one that failed. He kept on going, crossing the country promoting Pinterest, which took two years to catch on. There had to be moments during each step of the process when he wondered if he had made the right choice, yet he persevered and created a multi-billion dollar company.

A good friend Josh was working in finance in a small town in the Carolinas. He had a nice home, good income, wonderful family, and a group of people he had been friends with growing up. Life was good, yet he had always had the desire to work in film. After a long conversation with his wife Monica he decided to apply to film schools. It took a couple of years, but they moved to New York and he pursued his dream of attending grad school and becoming a filmmaker. Josh landed a job after graduation, but progress was slow at first and he was dogged by questions over whether he had done the right thing by uprooting his family and moving them to the city. They had traded a home with a nice yard for a small two bedroom apartment in Manhattan, his income had gone from that of a financier to one of an entry-level position in the film industry, his wife left the business she had started in their small town, and his daughter was being raised as a savvy New Yorker as opposed to a small town girl. You might be wondering how he could have made this choice and how Monica could have supported the idea. Well, she had dreams of her own. Moving to New York allowed her to focus more on her family and to work on an acting career. It seemed like a win-win, yet it took a while for Josh to begin producing the kind of projects he had gone to school to make. They had made enormous *Trades*, ones that would change their lives forever. They will never be able to live the same life they left behind, but now their days are filled with New York culture, Josh is working on projects with well-known talent, and their daughter loves her school and friends. As for Monica, you have already read about her. She is the woman in Chapter Two who decided to go back to grad school to get a degree in counseling and is now enjoying her newfound career. Their lives have been deeply changed by the *Trades* they made, and whatever comes next, they will have the satisfaction of having taken a chance and achieved their goals.

Whether in your personal life or business there is always a cost for each *Trade* that you make. A simple example is deciding to spend Saturday relaxing and binge-watching TV. The benefit would be quiet time at home relaxing and catching up on your favorite show. The cost could be not spending time with friends, getting outside, taking a class and learning a new skill, or writing your first screenplay. As you make choices throughout the day keep in mind your Twenty One Summers and the decisions that will bring you closer to them. Also keep in mind the opportunities lost, as they may be equally important if not more so.

Not making a choice has an impact too. Apple founder Steve Jobs gave up choice when it came to the famous black turtlenecks, jeans, and New Balance shoes he wore every day. Jobs believed that you have a limited amount of decision making power each day and that choosing clothes was a waste of time and energy. He benefited by saving time deciding what to wear, giving him more time and mental capacity to focus on his goals, but lost the ability to express himself in different ways. This is a small choice but the pathway to your Twenty One is filled with small *Trades* that add up to big changes.

Each of the decisions above includes a time component. Time is valuable because whether we are talking about the Twenty One Summers of your teens and twenties, forties and fifties, or those after retirement, time is all we have. The way that you decide to spend your time is at the crux of your Twenty One Summers and the only way to maximize time is by making *Trades*.

Andrew Hawken, who we initially met in Chapter Five, failed the 11 Plus test, a standardized problem solving exam that was given to students in the UK when they were 11 years old. When we last saw Andrew he had *Traded* a comfortable job at a small local newspaper for a chance to work at the United Kingdom's largest news organization, the BBC. During his ten years there he rose through the ranks ultimately producing the Nightly News and *Today*, the broadcaster's leading programs. The shows won numerous awards and Andrew found himself traveling the world working on stories with national and global importance. Running three and a half hours of live programming each night was both challenging and chaotic, but he got used to managing teams under extreme pressure. Despite his success, Andrew knew that he didn't want to spend the rest of his life with the BBC. As he said, "There are lots of people who have done this, they've had a lifelong career at the BBC and that's fine. But I didn't want that, didn't want to stay there forever."

Though he had spent his entire career telling stories, it was time for something different and that meant making a *Trade.* It was at that point he decided to go to Microsoft. Four years later he and his family moved to Seattle and

Andrew began working in the headquarters. This wasn't just a shift in process: it was a massive cultural shift. Suddenly Andrew was working with coders and engineers. He had stepped from the hectic pace of the newsroom into a world run by business plans, spreadsheets, and math. Though there were demands and pressure filled deadlines in both jobs, his skills were in a completely different area. He felt lost, wondering if he had made a mistake. As Andrew described, "I went through many moments thinking 'I have really screwed up my career big time,'" but once he got into the job he told himself "Hey, you know I've done this. I'm now going to make a success of it. The opportunity to be one of the pioneers in a very famous medium, I think that was incredibly exciting. It was a big motivation."

Andrew's teams at Microsoft were leaders in innovating the way content is consumed online. He created the first web portal which became www.msn.com. For years it was one of the most visited sites on the planet. The baseline technology they developed has since moved from portals to phones and other devices. The influence of his innovations can be traced all the way to TikTok.

Despite his success Andrew felt like an apple in a group of oranges, "I was always a content guy, an editor in chief. Then at Microsoft I had the chance to run the product development group and that was huge. Suddenly I've got one hundred strong Microsoft engineers working for me and I'm not a software guy. That was really challenging, but what I found out is that I can motivate teams. That, and I knew enough to surround myself with great people and that allowed the team to be successful." Yet Andrew's family wasn't happy in Seattle and wanted to move back to the UK. This meant another *Trade*, moving back to England and commuting to Seattle for work for the next two years. In the end he wanted to spend more time at home, so he left Microsoft and took a job running Sky News in London.

Then in 2016 Andrew saw a promising technology that offered new possibilities. He decided to take six months to a year away from his job at Sky to explore potential business opportunities and within a week he and his co-founder had launched Mesmerise, a company focused on virtual reality. This was four years before Mark Zuckerberg said virtual reality was going to be the focus at Meta. They have since successfully pivoted into AI and launched a joint venture called NeuRealities with the Mayo Clinic. With that announcement, Andrew's most recent *Trade* was done. The child who wasn't good enough for university has had a stellar career and is now leading a tech start-up developing one of technology's most promising innovations. There were a lot of *Trades* along the path from journalist to the founder of a tech company. A lot of opportunities for success and failure, but in the end, Andrew has proved himself to all doubters. That is truly inspiring. Don't let your or other people's doubts hold you back. You have the power to change your life.

Overcoming doubters doesn't have to happen on a grand scale. When I was young, my father always talked about having a pond with a little fountain in our backyard. One day his family was visiting for a holiday. I was probably eight years old, we were all sitting in the living room talking and he brought up his idea for the pond. His sister responded, "Oh stop, you're such a dreamer. It will never happen," to which I vehemently replied, "Don't say that. My Dad's not a dreamer. He's going to do it!" The response still surprises me to this day. It wasn't that I didn't believe in my Dad, I did deeply. I had just never talked to anyone in my family that way before and wasn't sure where the emotion came from. It was years later that he finally put in that little pond with a tiny fountain. I remember him taking me outside to show it off during a visit back home from college. I felt a deep sense of happiness and pride for him that day, and still do. It may have taken years, but he overcame the doubters and those who questioned him. I knew what the moment really meant to him, and in many ways to us. It was one of the first times that I realized our relationship was changing and though he was a *Pillar* in my life I was becoming one in his.

Questions around *Trades* arise on a business level as well a personal one. As we have seen, social perspectives, societal needs, and technology can change rapidly, making a substantial investment priceless or creating company defining losses. Just ask Kodak about film and their decision not to make the shift directly into digital technologies. The use of the Waterfall or Agile Process is another example of how a company's approach to business can make an enormous difference in its success. As we noted, the Agile Process permits companies to incorporate feedback and respond to changes in the world as they develop and release a service or product. It has also allowed companies like Mesmerise to shift focus and react to change. The Waterfall Process makes it difficult to respond to changes in society and technology due to its rigid timeline and inability to incorporate change into the decision making process.

The same thing applies to your choices. Don't hold rigidly on to a single pathway or way of making decisions.

Utilize the Agile Process after making a *Trade* and continue to learn, adapt to new opportunities, and incorporate new information. Be flexible and make adjustments that will keep you on track toward your Twenty One.

This is important, as every *Trade* inevitably alters the opportunities that follow it. Imagine each big decision as a point in time with thousands of lines radiating out from it, each line representing a different path or opportunity. The minute you make a decision, the lines from that point inevitably change and a new set of options take their place. The thread you choose to follow will lead to a new point with lines leading out from it. Some of these points in life are more substantial than others. They are moments of decision, change, or *Trades* that will alter your life forever. During these times, do not make rash or emotion filled decisions. Take a minute, slow down, evaluate the options available to you, and then take one step. Remember, your next step is just the first down a new pathway. Each step leads to a new series of threads and possibilities, allowing you to adjust your path along the way.

There are times when it may not seem as if there are any threads leading away from the place you are now and you may wonder how you will move forward and begin living life again. In these moments you have to choose a direction and take the first step, even a small step, toward one of your Twenty One. This may be the first time you exercise after life changing surgery, getting out of bed in the morning as you adjust to life after losing a loved one, making the first phone call to find new job after being laid off, applying to another school after not getting into the college you wanted to attend, rebuilding after a destructive weather event, or finding new communities after retiring.

These are just a few of the times when your pathway may appear cloudy and you may not feel like you have any options, but that first step is always there for you. A single action, one small change, is the start of transforming and revitalizing your life.

We met Hugh Williams in Chapter Three, an educator who decided to stay in Australia instead of taking a job with Google. Though it may have seemed like it, that wasn't the end of Hugh's story. He went on to make a series of *Trades* that have led to an extraordinary career and a satisfying Twenty One. A few years after turning down Google, Hugh said yes to a job with Microsoft. He flew to Seattle for a two day interview and decided that he wanted to work on their search engine Bing. He was now married, had two daughters, and was feeling the financial pressure of paying off a mortgage. His perspective had changed and the Blind Spots *Make Me Comfortable* and *Who Can I Be* that had kept him from Google were no longer at work. He wasn't sure if he was going to love the change, but he did know that he would be able to pay off his mortgage and that alone made it worthwhile. Success came quickly, perhaps too quickly. He enjoyed the projects and the challenge, but felt overwhelmed and a bit unsure of his ability to manage teams on a large scale.

That was when Christopher Payne, one of the original Corporate Vice Presidents at Microsoft, came into the picture. Payne had left Microsoft and launched a tech start-up that was bought by eBay. He was then tasked with making eBay profitable and wanted Hugh to run their search division. Christopher said, "It's going to be amazing. We can work really closely together. There are other people I could have picked but I picked you. You're the guy." That left Hugh facing another potential *Trade*: did he stay in Seattle at Microsoft, a safe and successful company where he was working with people he liked, or take a chance and move to California and a company that was facing a number of challenges at the time?

In a reversal of roles, his wife was against the move as their family had settled into Seattle, but eBay made an incredible offer and it was going to be a great career move. The company flew them both to their headquarters in California and closed the deal. Things went well at eBay, until a new CEO came on board and it became time for Hugh to leave. In Hugh's words, "Then I made one of the dumbest moves I've ever made. Honestly, I sort of panicked. I needed a job and made a decision based on the wrong criteria. I wanted money, a fancy title, and I wanted to run an entire tech team, which is the worst criteria ever to base a decision on." His next job was an awful experience. The company was disorganized and he never did get to run the entire tech team. In short, the environment was toxic. As we know from Chapter Three, when you find yourself in those situations it is time to move on, and Hugh did.

Once again, Christopher Payne entered Hugh's life. Christopher had just been named the CEO of Tinder and wanted to hire Hugh, but it was going to take a while to make that happen. Hugh waited for two months, wondering daily if the call would ever come. It finally did and he was asked to run the entire tech team at the Los Angeles based company. It meant another move, but they went. Three months later, Christopher was let go from Tinder and Hugh had a decision to make. A loyal friend had been fired and he felt staying was the wrong thing to do, so he left the company and was unemployed once again leaving him wondering what the next *Trade* would be.

As we have often noted, the *Trades* in your life may not be large, but they may be substantial to you. Even the smallest decisions can alter your work/life balance. Once you realize that life is made up of *Trades* it will be a little easier to compare your options and make decisions. There is always a cost and a benefit; when you understand that your choices will become clearer.

A hard lesson for many of us is that we are responsible for the *Trades* that we make. It is important to be accountable for your choices, good and bad. Do not get lost in rationalizations or beat yourself up when things don't go well. We all make bad *Trades* from time to time. Remember Derrick's thirty million dollar mistake at Microsoft? With each mistake, the *Walls of Your Knowledge* expand giving you a new understanding and perspective that you can apply in the future. As long as you learn and grow from your mistakes, they can be invaluable, but if you consistently make bad choices then you need to stop, take a look at yourself, review your Blind Spots, and ask why you are doing things that hold you back. Don't make excuses, as we have said before they are boring and no one wants to hear them. They may be the only thing keeping you from being honest with yourself and achieving your Twenty One.

The first step toward better decision making has to come from within. You have the power to affect change in your life and the responsibility for your choices lies with you.

In my third year of high school, I had chemistry class with Mr. Hugdahl. Each week he gave us a quiz and when he returned them the following Monday he wrote how many people got each grade on the blackboard. He didn't include people's names, just the number of people who received an A, B, C, D or F. For some reason, I could remember what Mr. Hugdahl presented in class during the week and got As on the quizzes without having to study. One week, I was sick and missed three days of class. He sent the reading and homework to my house, but I had developed some bad habits over the course of the semester and didn't really study them. When Mr. Hugdahl returned the quizzes the next week he stopped at my desk and as he put the quiz down said, "Mr. Werner, you pay the fiddler, you dance the tune." I didn't get an A that week, but the lesson learned was far greater than chemistry. It was that I was responsible for my actions and that for every *Trade* in life there would be a response. It was inevitable, whether I wanted there to be one or not. If I didn't put in the work I wouldn't get the desired result. Sometimes life is that simple.

"You pay the fiddler, you dance the tune" is a small phrase, but one that I often hear him saying when I haven't done the necessary work or have made a *Trade* that wasn't a good one. It reminds me that in the end I am accountable for my choices. Ultimately, whether I reach any of my Twenty One is up to me and the amount of effort that I put in along the way. A large part of that is managing my time, developing new habits, making good *Trades*, working to understand and overcome my Blind Spots, and always taking a step forward even when life pushes back.

We all deserve success and a good work/life balance, but as we noted above what that balance is will be different for each of us. I worked hard for six or seven days a week to develop a life and career that would allow me to create and travel. Derrick chose to spend close to one hundred hours a week working at Microsoft, a *Trade* that he was glad to make as he enjoyed the work that he was doing. In return, he was able to develop products that affect many of our lives. It also allowed him to retire and be able to travel and explore fashion photography, snowboarding, and downhill biking. The *Trades* he made while working affected his social life and took up any extra time that he had, but those choices have now given him the opportunity to explore his interests fully along with doing some consulting and co-authoring this book. You could argue that Derrick's work/life balance was off for many years, and many people did, but he loved his work and for him it was an easy *Trade* to make. You don't need to work six days or one hundred hours a week to achieve all of your goals, but the time and effort you put in will go a long way toward defining the lifestyle you'll be able to live and how many of your Twenty One you are able to reach.

Remember Elinor the photographer we met in Chapter Three? She *Traded* the comfort of her life at home to move to the United States and take on the dream of seeing her photographs published in a book. Elinor has also *Traded* a certain amount of privacy to tell us beautiful and poignant stories that are deeply personal yet universal. Glimpses into her and her family's private life address the ideas, experiences, and rituals of family, intimacy, marriage, motherhood, and mid-life. Each of her family members choose when and how they share their lives in her photographs. These are *Trades* they all make on a regular basis. For Elinor, work and family life often blend, at times becoming one and the same. It is an appropriate work/life balance for her and her family.

Your *Trades* will involve other people too whether they are family members, friends, or colleagues at work and play. The effect your choices have on those around you is unavoidable. Most people we know strive to keep their work and personal life separate. Others find them to be almost inseparable with their profession demanding exceptional discipline and an integrated lifestyle to achieve. Each is a valid choice. As we noted earlier, be sure that those around you understand the work/life balance you want or need. Include them in conversations about your goals and the *Trades* you need to make to reach them.

Regularly taking the time to sit down and redefine your Twenty One will help you find a work/life balance that makes sense. As you do so, pay particular attention to the *Trades* that you have made and those you are considering. Be sure that they are moving you toward your Twenty One and not away from them. Check to see if you are managing your time effectively or if you are using excuses and poor time management to *Make Yourself Comfortable*. Be honest with yourself. Bad time management is a device that people commonly use to avoid taking on the important things in life.

Discuss your findings with good friends, a family member, your book club, or one of the *Stars* in your life. Doing so will help you understand the anchors that are holding you back and may need to be part of your next series of *Trades.* It will also help you clarify your priorities and find a balance between your personal life, work demands, and your goals.

Chapter Seven
The Crossover

It was the beginning of 2019, and I thought that my life was set. I had worked for years to build a career in which I would be able to travel, teach, and create. After working in Russia I knew there were opportunities abroad and I wanted to develop new projects internationally. Two Chinese businesswomen were interested in collaborating on projects in Europe, the United States, and China.

The first woman proposed bringing Chinese students and educators to New York for educational workshops and putting together a six city series of talks with universities and private art schools in China. The second was interested in putting together a workshop that combined business and culture to be offered in seven countries in Europe, in addition to China and possibly Saint Petersburg, Russia.

The first three week workshop in New York was set to happen in July of that year. I had found rooms and instructors, developed curriculum, and had a schedule set for tours of the city. This was going to be the stepping off point to a new career, one that I had been building toward for years. A week before the workshop, the organizer called to say that it would not be happening. I was crushed, the cancellation of the project was going to be a large personal financial loss and, though the six city speaking tour happened, it did not look like we were going to be able to pursue new projects together in the future. I took the time set aside for the New York workshop to travel to my hometown, put things in storage, and spend time with family and friends as the second client and I discussed the China and Europe based project. In early February of 2020 I left for Italy, where our team was set to meet in Rome and Florence to team build, tighten up the curriculum, and develop promotional materials. I had never been to Italy so I went a few days early to explore the country. On the way back to Rome, my business partner called to say that their Lufthansa flight had been canceled and they were not letting people out of China. It was the beginning of the pandemic and the end of our business together.

At that moment, I realized that I had gone from the precipice of my dream job to no work at all. Everything had been shut down, all of the teaching, public speaking, workshops, travel, were gone. I was hardly alone in this moment. Many businesses were facing similar challenges, but that did not change the situation. Upon getting back to the United States I sat at home and wondered what I was going to do. My Twenty One Summers had been taken apart and I couldn't imagine a new set of goals. Then I realized, it was time for *The Crossover.*

The Crossover begins with honestly evaluating your existing skills and then finding new ways to apply them as you look for and create new opportunities for yourself. This means stepping away from your normal assumptions and solutions to look objectively at yourself and what is happening in life. Your immediate response to a situation like the one above may be to just see loss, to look for a new job in the same field or, given the pandemic to take whatever position might be available. These are all valid responses, but none use *The Crossover.* There is a phrase,

"When one door closes another one opens." The reality is the next door doesn't always open by itself; you have to open it and be prepared when it does. Really, there are a set of doors that you can open with each leading to a different lifestyle or opportunity. Most people will not consider the majority of those doors, only opening the door that is most familiar.

During challenging times, we often default to old ways of thinking, believing that we are defined by our history, a job, town, community, relationship, or another event or object. The Blind Spots *Who Am I*, *Who Am I Supposed To Be*, *Who Can I Be*, *Make Me Comfortable*, *Yes, But Who Am I Really*, and *Knowledge As A Wall* all come rushing back to play their roles, limiting the options we envision. We begin to question our ability as these Blind Spots keep us from creating new definitions of ourselves, leaving us unable to see or value skills that we often overlook or take for granted. The new threads of life emanating out from these points may seem few, but you neither have to go back to old ways of living nor start from scratch. You are your most valuable asset and it is time to use that asset to its fullest. Though you may find it hard to envision new ways of applying even your best skills, the goal of *The Crossover* is to help you do so.

Mark was interested in creating well researched, compassionate, and insightful photo documentaries. Hard working, he always strove to put together a compelling narrative and get the story right. His last year of school he spent weeks living at and around the United States border with Mexico. In doing so, he found a way to spend time riding along with the US Border Patrol, getting to know the leader and participants in an anti-immigration group working in the region, and photographing pro-immigration supporters as well. Each person that he interviewed or photographed for the story felt respected and heard, that is not an easy thing to do. One of Mark's talents as a photographer is his ability to get access to the people and locations necessary to be successful and to foster trust between himself and his subjects. This along with his honesty and authenticity are invaluable skills.

Despite his dedication to photography, life as a documentary photographer was challenging and getting stories published was a long path, so he decided to apply for a job as a photo editor and ultimately became a Senior Photo Editor at the New York Daily News. The transition made sense as it would allow him to apply his knowledge as an image maker as he assigned photographers and selected photos to run in the newspaper. It felt good to be able to give photographers work, and he had a chance to make a difference as the audience was large and he could try to bring his Core Values of honesty and integrity to the job.

There are a number of challenges to working as a Photo Editor at a newspaper in a city the size of New York. Like all jobs, you answer to a series of bosses who have input into what you do. Mark's bosses selected the stories that the newspaper would cover and often had strong opinions regarding the photographs that would be used to illustrate certain stories. That, in addition to the often brutal nature of the news in the city, became exhausting. Ethics are central to the news and there were constant questions regarding what photographs should be run, especially those that were extremely personal or gruesome in nature. Over time, the job wore on Mark and he decided to move to Santa Fe, New Mexico where he rested and recuperated personally and emotionally, detoxing from the news that had surrounded him. It was there that *The Crossover* really came into play. He had used his skills as a photographer to transition into his role as an editor, that was a logical move, but what were his options in a rather small New Mexican town?

Mark considered working as a photographer again but the pure joy that had accompanied his early work was missing. It was then he decided to become an Emergency Medical Technician (EMT), entering the Santa Fe Fire Department's academy as one of the older recruits. This may seem a world away from his work as a photographer, but if you look at Mark's core traits you'll realize it was a natural progression, one that utilizes *The Crossover.* Mark had always been hard working, compassionate and driven in large part to help others, whether it was telling their story or assigning someone a job at the newspaper. His stories sought to bring understanding to the world and ultimately a positive message. Helping others as an EMT gave him the opportunity to put these traits to use on a daily basis, benefiting those he came in contact with and providing a deep sense of personal satisfaction. The talent that allowed him to gain access to situations, put people at ease, and build a sense of trust, all come into play when the team confronts difficult situations or he needs to gain the trust of someone as he treats their injuries. These skills, along with a sense of leadership honed in the newsroom, make him a great teammate at the Fire Department.

Mark may not be utilizing the hard skills such as using a camera and working in Photoshop that were important as a photographer or editor, but his soft skills like the personality traits and interpersonal skills that have always been part of his work are central to his new role. Hard skills can often be learned, but soft skills such as leadership and clear communication can be far more difficult to master, yet they are often the key to transitioning from one job or lifestyle to another.

When you find yourself on the verge of a transition in life take stock of your soft skills as well as your hard skills. Make a list of the things that drive you, the personal traits that have helped you succeed in the past, and the core beliefs that you value. Then make a list of your hard skills, the technical and physical skills that you have, as well as the knowledge gained from work, school, volunteering, or life experience. Look at your lists from a fresh perspective and imagine the places those skills might apply. Perhaps discuss them with a *Star,* family member, your book club, or friend. Like Mark, you may find your talent or calling in an area that you never imagined.

Rosie is a Niger based mother of five, an award winning women's and education activist, and one of Africa's leading women and girls' rights advocates. She is currently the Deputy Director of Programs at the International Rescue Committee in Niger managing the organization's portfolio and a team of over one hundred fifty. I had the pleasure of meeting Rosie while teaching at the United Nations Education First Summer School, where her energy and kindness stood out in a room of ninety two young leaders from around the world selected from over fourteen thousand applications. A friend and bit of a hero of mine, I find Rosie a rather extraordinary person: she has a humbleness and comfortable dedication to her not for profit work that is inspiring.

It is a humbleness that belies the challenges of working in Africa's male centric governments and the social unrest that has seen her survive internal strife in her home country of Cameroon, and three coups d'etats, moving her family as she adjusted to each change. Yet I have never heard Rosie complain about the challenges she has faced. There are conversations to be sure, but she is always looking for a solution, for the next step on her pathway, and for that she has my deepest respect.

When we met Rosie was working in Cameroon's major cities, remote villages, and at times across the African continent. Much of her time was spent visiting tribes that can only be reached by hiking into the bush. Her efforts have always been focused on the empowerment of women on a national, local, and tribal level, helping women and young girls understand that they have choices in life that include education, owning a business, the right to have their voices heard, and options other than child marriage. In many of these areas, tribal language does not provide a word for a woman's private parts nor for menstruation, making it difficult to help women understand the need for healthier and more sanitary practices and to remove the shame that often accompanies a woman's period in these regions.

For Rosie, achieving her goals often meant overcoming decades or centuries of belief systems and traditions. To that end, she develops educational programs that teach women how to run a business making soap and other sanitary goods that remove the stigma of menstruation and provide a pathway toward personal and financial independence. Rosie also strives to reserve time for women to speak in front of local governing councils. For most women, this is the first time that they have been heard by local or tribal leaders. That validation alone makes a difference in each individual's life and that of the village.

All of the Blind Spots that we've discussed are active in the countries, towns, and villages that Rosie works in. *Who Am I, Who Am I Supposed To Be, Who Can I Be, Make Me Comfortable, Yes, But Who Am I Really, Knowledge As A Wall*, and *The Trade* are each impacting women's lives. By identifying the challenges facing these women and taking the first step toward a sustainable solution, Rosie is able to develop a plan of action that blossoms from a series of small steps into larger initiatives that ripple outward, changing people's lives and providing new opportunities. It takes a coordinated effort on an individual and societal level to provide solutions that move women past the Blind Spots that have been holding them back. For Rosie these are solutions that empower, helping everyone in the village live fuller, healthier, and more satisfying lives.

You can use the same process as Rosie as you take on your Twenty One. Begin by clearly and concisely identifying the initial challenge and/or goal. Do your research and build a better understanding of your options, even those that are initially outside the *Walls of Your Knowledge.* Look at any obstacles with an eye toward potential solutions, not as reasons for defeat. Allow your perspective to change and beliefs to evolve as you identify and work on your Blind Spots. Then take tangible action based on what you have learned, making small manageable steps along the way with each action building on the last. Adjust your pathway as new challenges arise or positive changes occur, and finally, celebrate each step forward and the goals large and small accomplished along the way.

At first, Rosie's *Crossover* may seem less obvious than most. She hasn't faced a career change like Mark has, but the traits that make her an extraordinary friend, mother and wife *Crossover* to help make her a true humanitarian. If you have the desire to help others or to work for a not for profit, then soft skills like communication, compassion, building trust, belief in opportunity and equality, and advocating for others are important. These, along with hard skills like Rosie's strength as a project manager, producer, and grant writer, are a combination that may resonate with you as they will allow you to bring change to the world.

These are hundreds of reasons *The Crossover* might need to happen in your life. It may not seem like it at the time, but change, loss, or instability often create opportunity. The challenge is to find that opportunity and incorporate it into your Twenty One.

There are times when I have found myself questioning my role and relevance or working successfully and wondering whether I was putting too much time and effort into a single goal to the exclusion of other opportunities. This has been a reoccurring question in my life, part of a constant recalibration of life choices and goals that have consciously and subconsciously become a component of my daily and weekly routine. These are a series of mental check-ins on my personal and career choices, my diet and health, work/life balance, individual projects like writing this book, or asking myself whether to say yes or no to additional projects. It is an effort to keep life aligned with my Twenty One and to see if I need to make a *Trade*, *Crossover*, or another adjustment.

Even with frequent check-ins, there are moments when change can catch us by surprise. One day I was asked to speak about business in a friend's class at a university in New York. It was the third day back after a holiday break and the students were taking a while to settle in and focus. As my friend struggled to get the students to pay attention, it hit me that I never wanted to work full time in academia again. I love teaching and still enjoy teaching classes and workshops, giving lectures, consulting, and working with people one on one, but in that brief second I knew that my desire to continue a full time teaching career was over. It was a powerful and disorienting moment. I didn't know what I was going to do next or what form my career would take. I certainly wasn't ready to retire, it was far too early in life for that, but I knew that chapter was done and *The Crossover* was going to be in play.

Changes like retirement are predetermined for most people. I hear friends and colleagues talk about retirement and what they imagine they will do, but I always wonder how the hobbies they talk about will fill their next twenty one or thirty years. If you're on the verge of retirement, think about everything that happened in your life from the day you were born until you were twenty one or thirty. You have that same amount of time ahead of you after retirement. Strive to stay physically and mentally vital and engaged. Work to make the quality of life in retirement as close as possible to the years that preceded it. Give your life a beautiful ending; let it be as extraordinary as you did when you were younger, or even more so.

Change is not always easy. Letting go of being a student or the person at the factory who was always part of the gang can be hard. Many retirees imagine having the same relevance in life and business as they had prior to retirement, but that inevitably changes. At some point, the person chairing black tie galas is moved from table one to table thirty four. A few years after retirement, the mortgage banker will not know everyone in town and the school secretary will not know all of the children. The things that have defined you are an important part of your history, but they will fade in your mind and more quickly in those of others. In this moment, it is important to redefine yourself, embrace new roles, *Crossover,* and apply your knowledge in new ways. Don't let your Blind Spots hold you back, or worse, slowly take away your motivation and cause depression.

Remember that you are far more vital and relevant than the titles that have defined you. This is essential as you move toward the next phase in life, whether that is retirement, a new place in your career, or a change in your personal life. It is another reason to regularly check in and update your Twenty One. Think of your Twenty One as a guidebook or pathway that will allow you to step into the next part of your life with a sense of purpose, however you define it.

In 2003, Derrick was working in London overseeing a team focused on the development and management of internet services for Microsoft in Europe. As mentioned in Chapter Six, at that point in his career he was looking for new ways to continue to grow. The obvious options were to make a lateral move to a team in London, join an engineering team at Microsoft's US headquarters, or move to a different company. The fourth option was to combine the first two choices and move to a different division at the company's US headquarters. This choice was risky because he was comfortable in his current position. As Derrick noted, "I had a strong identity in the industry and there was a potential for failure that would have diminished my reputation and could have destroyed my career." Unsure of what to do, he reached out to a *Mentor* at the company who supported his idea, so when an opportunity surfaced to run the marketing team for Microsoft's Search Investments, Derrick was interested. There were several reasons he might not get the position. First and foremost, Derrick did not have any experience in marketing and the skill sets needed were different from those in his current position. Engineering required deep technical skills while marketing required creativity, communication and an understanding of your audience. In addition, the job change would mean a step down the corporate ladder. Even so, Derrick decided to apply for the job, "I had to. I had to find a way to differentiate myself from the other five hundred engineers." How was he going to have a chance to get the position? By using *The Crossover*.

Since Derrick didn't have any experience in marketing, he promoted the skills he felt *Crossed Over* to the new role during the interview. One of his initial suggestions was to apply the Agile Process used in product development in the marketing department. The goal was to make the company's marketing efforts more flexible, rolling out new features on a regular basis and becoming more responsive to customer feedback as it came in. It made sense as the marketing department was still operating under the Waterfall Process, using linear longer term planning with marketing gaps between large product releases. They had not adjusted to the speed of online marketing and the change in their company's product development timeline. Derrick's years of internet focused product development had given him a unique understanding of how online search and the Agile Process worked, as well as the ways they might be applied in the marketing division. He also focused on his leadership experience and team management skills. His expertise there would allow him to work closely with seasoned marketing experts while challenging them to evaluate their methodology and metrics for success. Derrick also had a depth of experience integrating teams while focusing their effort on new and evolving challenges, which was exactly what marketing needed. Finally, his career as an engineer had been defined in large part by his drive to problem solve, a drive that is essential in marketing where you have to continually find creative solutions.

By acknowledging his lack of experience in marketing and focusing on the soft skills and experience that *Crossed Over* to the marketing team, Derrick got the job. It would have been easy to come up with reasons not to apply, but it was far harder to honestly and objectively look at his skills and find ways they were realistically applicable to the new position. Though it took time for him to grow into the role, he won over the team. After three years, he moved back into research and development at a more senior level, bringing along a unique skill set. He was no longer one of five hundred. The time spent learning marketing made him a much stronger product development leader. Derrick's experience also made him a more attractive candidate for jobs at Microsoft's headquarters, especially at higher levels of management that necessitated interacting with divisions across the company.

The idea that a single skill set is the most direct pathway to success is still prevalent in many companies and communities. Though slowly diminishing in everyday practice, the notion that we have a singular option in terms of our career is reinforced by our educational system and many of the businesses for which we work. Careers are rarely linear. Life, skills, and opportunities change and we make adjustments along the way.

As we discussed in Chapter Two, educators often decide at an early age whether we are creative, good in STEM, and even whether we are intelligent or not. We are often viewed, and view ourselves, through that lens for the remainder of our basic education if not our lives. The impressions that people have of you can hold you back, potentially keeping you from a career that you may love and excel in. Don't let those impressions define you or defeat you.

The impressions that we hold on to from our childhood are not only centered around creativity or whether you have an aptitude for science or technology. We filter our experiences through comments from individuals, groups, businesses, family, and communities for our entire lives. If an individual or a group of people told you that you were not smart, should not travel, or didn't deserve success, you might filter all of your choices and opportunities through those comments. Any personal, social, or cultural comments, ideas or beliefs can become a filter through which you perceive everything that happens in your life, hindering your ability to *Expand The Walls of Your Knowledge*, learn *Who Can I Be*, answer *Yes, But Who Am I Really*, make objectively thought out *Trades*, and see the advantages of *The Crossover*. Over the long term, the words you hear repeatedly as a child or adult can become Blind Spots that need to be overcome so that you can live your life to its greatest potential.

As noted earlier, we are generally taught that the skills we learn are only applicable to one or perhaps two job categories, yet many of your hard and soft skills *Crossover* into a variety of fields. This is not something that is often discussed in school. This is due in part to the disappearance of liberal studies degrees that promoted the study of a broad range of topics, in part to curriculum that inhibits true real world and cross-program collaboration, and in part to educators who are deeply invested in holding on to traditional methods of teaching or are concerned about job security. Increasing levels of administration in education and the oversight that has come with it impedes flexibility in terms of programming and teachers who promote real entrepreneurial exploration in the classroom. It also diminishes a student's ability to learn and apply their talent and knowledge across a number of areas as opposed to a single pursuit. For many people, teachers included, it is easier to put people in a box and define them with a single label than to view them with a broader vision and foster their growth.

This singularity can be problematic as a job in your field of study may not materialize, leaving you facing a range of unexpected limitations, or opportunities that demand a range of skills.

Parents, teachers, counselors, family, and friends all have definitions of *Who You Are* and *Who You Can Be*. You were the student, the athlete, the artist, the mathematician, the partier, the outdoors person, the quiet introvert, the fashionable extrovert. These labels can feel good and we often work hard to define ourselves by them. Doing so helps us find community, stand out among our peers, and make those around us comfortable with who we are. We try to live up to them, good or bad, and let them depict who we are, how we act, and who we are supposed to be. We also let them limit our choices. The major that you chose in college may be due in large part to how people defined you or a label that you held on to. Maybe your job was chosen the same way. You were always supposed to be the artist, the coder, the accountant, because everyone told you that was what you are good at or that is what you should be.

It is interesting how we are frequently told what we should do or cannot do but are seldom told that our hard and soft skills may apply across multiple interests or professions. We limit ourselves as well, rarely looking outside the *Walls of Our Knowledge* or making a *Crossover* to find out what our options might be. The Blind Spots *Make Me Comfortable, Who Am I* and *Who Am I Supposed To Be*, are part of our educational systems, relationships, businesses, and communities, as well as our personal lives. Don't let them hold you back. Stay aware, stay awake, keep your love for life alive even during the hard times, and know that you have the power to bring about change in your life and the lives of others.

It is important to note that we are not dismissing the fact that you need a depth of knowledge and a strong skill set to compete for a job and to do it effectively. Whatever you decide to do you should be well prepared and ready to do it to the best of your ability. Diversifying is important, but if you work in more than one field you need to do both well. In fact, you need to excel. Whether we are talking about Derrick's ability to move to marketing and then back to leading engineering teams and developing new ways for the world to engage online while at Microsoft, or my time as the Director of the Photography Program at Parsons, getting a master's degree, working in Russia, and running an art gallery in New York at the same time, working hard and delivering at a high level allowed us the flexibility to take on diverse responsibilities.

Hugh Williams, formerly of Google, eBay, Tinder, Microsoft, and a consultant to the CEO of DoorDash, would say that if you work hard and take chances you will create more opportunities for yourself. The more opportunities that you create, the greater the probability that things will work out for you. He has lived that throughout his life and career.

When we left Hugh in Chapter Six, he had just made an enormous *Trade*, finding himself unemployed after leaving his job at Tinder out of loyalty to his friend Christopher Payne. Christopher had moved to DoorDash and did ask Hugh to come on board, but the company was struggling at the time so Hugh decided to use *The Crossover* instead. He took a job running Google Maps, a completely new area of expertise for him. Despite the new job at Google, Hugh and Christopher's lives were going to cross again. DoorDash was a success under Christopher's management and he finally hired Hugh as a consultant. This *Crossover* has been a success for everyone involved. It had been a long demanding path from the University to DoorDash. A lot of *Trades* had been made, as Hugh expanded the *Walls of His Knowledge* and regularly redefined *Who Am I, Who Can I Be, Make Me Comfortable, and Who Am I Really* while working toward an ever evolving Twenty One.

A few years later, Hugh and his wife were hiking in the California hills and they realized it was time to move back home to Australia, but before that could happen there was one more *Crossover* that needed to take place. Hugh had been lucky enough to learn coding as a child and a college student in Australia and he wanted others from his homeland to have the same opportunity. He and his wife decided it was time to give back. Applying all of his skills in management and technology, they started a charity that helps secondary school teachers teach children how to code. The benefits of the project are twofold as it allows teachers to develop new skills and add to their existing salary while helping students explore new ideas and learn skills that will make them more relevant in the future. This is all done with an eye toward introducing students to *Teachers* and *Mentors*, expanding the *Walls of Their Knowledge*, and giving them a new point of view when they ask *Who Am I* and *Who Can I Be*. In its first year, the foundation ran classes in eight schools teaching eight hundred and forty students. This year they are funding classes in more than two hundred schools with over fifty five thousand students attending. This is a *Crossover* that benefits everyone. Sometimes you have to walk away from everything to find the good things life has in store for you, and your true Twenty One.

According to the Bureau of Labor Statistics the average person in the United States has twelve jobs over the course of their lifetime. Some of those job changes may be early on when people are in school or trying to decide what they want to do, but the fact is more people are changing jobs mid-career and later in life. There are times when they move into similar positions and related fields and other times when they utilize *The Crossover* to explore new careers. Whether our own choice or an unexpected change these moments can happen to us all. You need to keep moving beyond the *Walls Of Your Knowledge* and make the *Trades* necessary to prepare yourself for new opportunities that may arise, or opportunities that you create on your own. Be ready to redefine *Who Can I Be* and *Yes, But Who Am I Really* as you rebuild, replenish, or redefine your life and your Twenty One.

Rebuilding was exactly what I had to do after the pandemic had wiped out all of my work. I found the need to use *The Crossover* ironic as I had just redefined myself, finding new ways to apply my skill sets in collaborations with Chinese partners. The international workshops we had planned combined much of my previous experience; teaching at a university, partnering with educational institutions and cultural centers, developing curriculum, managing projects, working globally, and so much more. Now just months later I needed to come up with a new way to apply my knowledge. It felt like life's greatest challenge, bigger than moving to New York, starting an art gallery, running the photo program at a university, or building out a network and working in Russia. They all paled in comparison to the task at hand. Friends were supportive saying that it would all be OK, that I had evolved throughout my career and always landed on my feet. Their comments were deeply appreciated and made a difference, but for a few months I could not see the answer.

As you know, my situation had been complicated by a double pulmonary embolism on a flight to the United States from China in late 2019. After the stay in the hospital I thought that my body had completely healed. The event seemed to be a one time issue, so two weeks later I headed back to China. Friends and acquaintances suggested sending someone else in my place, but as those of you who work for yourselves know, people hire you for specific reasons. Whether teaching, consulting, or working with clients one on one there is no one else to send. You, your talent, knowledge, insight, way of working, and ability to effect change is what people are looking for, and I appreciate and respect that idea.

The trip also offered the chance to expand my network, foster new relationships, and explore potential collaborations. This is something I had built my career upon, utilizing one opportunity to develop the next. I had regularly met physical and mental challenges while traveling and approached this trip in the same manner as usual. The one acknowledgment I gave to the embolism was to take a wheelchair from gate to gate at the airport while flying to China. During the first connection I stopped at an airline lounge and when standing up to check in fell back into the wheelchair. At that point I began to realize healing was going to take much longer than expected and I needed to take care during the trip.

If you have ever traveled to China for business you know that the Chinese can be extraordinary hosts. That meant luxurious dinners every night and entertainment before or after. I had to excuse myself at the end of each evening knowing my hosts wondered why I did not take greater advantage of their generosity, but sleep was essential. Upon returning to the States, I found the trip left me exhausted and with a serious case of Covid, one that added to the challenge.

The workshops in Europe and China were canceled in February of 2020 and the last bit of in person teaching fashion photography at New York Film Academy ended well. A lot had happened over the prior months and there was a lot of change to process in a short period of time.

Processing was one thing, but waiting was another. Each day that passed without work, without creating, without knowing what was going to happen next was hard to take, so I sat down and began *The Crossover* and the pathway back to reinventing my life and career.

Starting over again meant a tremendous amount of trust in myself and my skills, something that I was doubting at the time. *Who Can I Be* and *Yes, But Who Am I Really* were hard at work. Despite past success none of the usual solutions fit. I wasn't sure if I was ready for the challenge but I didn't have a choice, it had to happen. It was time to step back, objectively evaluate my skills, and look for new ways that they could be applied. One of my main goals, my Core Twenty One, became to consider every career choice that I had any interest in. I did not want to have any regrets. The book Twenty One Summers arose from that moment. I didn't know if, how, or when this book would be written, but I did know that one day before life was done, I wanted to make it happen.

Public speaking, moderating panel discussions and interviewing people on stage were strengths, but travel wasn't a possibility and the events that I used to speak at had been canceled. There was a need for content during Covid and a podcast seemed to be the perfect step toward utilizing my interviewing skills. So I ordered the equipment from Amazon, set up a makeshift studio and launched Thomas Werner Projects Podcast interviewing leaders from across creative fields who have crossed boundaries and built projects and careers that most only imagine. I spent hours learning the software and editing the talks. It was great to connect with people that I admired and share their experiences with a new audience. The idea was to give others insight into how they too could make a change in their lives and apply *The Crossover.* That alone was inspiring.

I also began to give online talks and teach workshops on topics that I knew well such as, *Publishing Your Own Book, Selling Your Fine Art and Alternatives to Galleries, Social Media Marketing for Creatives, The Business of Fine Art Photography,* and even *Launching a Podcast,* something I had just learned. These presentations kept me fresh and allowed me to get a sense of the knowledge and experience people were looking for, as well as how I could provide it. Each talk was based on a combination of feedback from people that I knew in the field, organizations that I had been a member of, or boards I had served on. It was like using the Agile Process on a much smaller scale in my personal life and business by responding to the information received from learning, listening, reaching out to others, and seeing how the world responded to my efforts.

The Crossover not only necessitates taking stock of your skills, but also the relationships and credibility you have established. My work commercially and with not for profits opened the door to presentations and audiences that helped rebuild and sustain my career. When giving talks I made sure to provide each organization and their members with information and insight that they could apply in their lives and careers. They knew that they could trust my ability to deliver because I had done so in the past.

Trust and credibility are built over time. When you have a track record of delivering what you promise on time and on budget people will be more comfortable working with you. This becomes invaluable when you need to use *The*

Crossover. If you are just starting out, you can build on smaller successes. Showing up, being on time, learning new skills, staying positive, being prepared, and over delivering on what you have promised, can go a long way toward establishing credibility. Not doing these things can go a long way toward destroying it.

Personally, I am not good at reaching out for help and seldom ask for favors. *Make Me Comfortable* hinders me in this area as I feel good about being self-sufficient. This was one time that I had to overcome my discomfort and to learn how to ask for help with humbleness and grace. Equally important, to do so in a way that helped move everyone involved forward. There were some people who welcomed the collaboration and others who did not. That will be part of the process when you are addressing any of your Blind Spots or working toward your Twenty One. There will be people who simply do not want to help. There may be several reasons for that and it is better to accept their choice and move on than to get angry. Your time is better spent moving past the people who want to hinder you than getting into the mud and fighting with them.

The next step was to launch TWP Creative Edge. Drawing on my personal network I offered opportunities to study one on one with leaders from various fields ranging from an Emmy Award Winning Producer to the former Creative Director at Snap, the company that founded Snapchat. The genesis of this idea came from the increasing cost of higher education and belief that in many creative fields the pathway to a career does not need to mean four or more years in higher education. Practical knowledge and a real world understanding of how creative industries work is hard to come by, but each of the mentors was willing to help their students realize potential pathways into the career of their choice.

We promoted Creative Edge internationally, but to my surprise the students signed up to work with me directly. The fact that people did not take advantage of the access to an extraordinary roster of mentors will forever confound me, but a number of important lessons were learned. First, value yourself, you are your greatest asset. Trust yourself and focus on your strengths, they are what others value as well. Visibility matters, you can be incredibly talented but if people do not know that you or your talent exists opportunities will not come your way. Do not get angry if your ideas do not work. You may put a lot of effort into things that are not successful, but as we saw with Pinterest, each idea is a gateway to the next.

During this entire process I was writing the book *The Business of Fine Art Photography* for Bloomsbury Publishing in London. As a writer you receive an advance but you do not get paid by a publisher while you write, so while the extra time was welcome the book was not generating any revenue. In early 2020 Bloomsbury sold their entire photography book division along with my contract to Routledge and I spent four months wondering if the book was going to be canceled. Uncertainty it seemed was the norm. Thankfully, Routledge said they wanted to move forward with publication, and I got back to writing again. It was a huge relief.

The podcast, talks, and TWP Creative Edge gave me visibility and continued credibility during a time when others were sitting still. The individual clients from Creative Edge led to a focus on consulting and working with individuals one on one, providing tools and information that gave them a chance to expand their business, further their education, or begin their own *Crossover*. As the consulting business grew clients from around the world began to reach out. People were looking for ways to develop new skills and add revenue streams to existing businesses, it was the perfect application for my skills. I was now building a new business internationally but in a way that I could not have imagined before. *The Crossover* was working. Overall business was stop and start, but there was momentum and after a few months I could see the pathway back to a new career and a redesigned Twenty One.

As Covid subsided and things started to open up, New York Film Academy began to run in person classes again and I was asked if I would teach a one on one class in fashion photography to a gentleman from Microsoft, which is what led Derrick and me to our conversations in Seattle and the beginning of this book. It is all tied together. If I hadn't lost the collaborations with my Chinese partners and applied *The Crossover,* Derrick and I would never have met and this book wouldn't have happened. An unexpected opportunity and friendship came from a time in life that did not seem to have a path forward.

One way or another, we all face these moments in life, times when we have to make life work or we give up. It may be due to an illness, an accident, an injury, sudden financial hardship, the loss of a loved one or a job; there are an endless number of unexpected challenges in life that change things forever. Despite our greatest efforts we cannot control everything, and maybe that is a good thing. For me, life had cleared the table. It took a while to realize what a gift that was as I was able to let go of old ways of thinking, reset, and try things I had never imagined doing.

During the writing process, a colleague and I were having coffee in New York one day and he asked for a little career advice. While giving him a few suggestions I related some of the stories in this book. He responded with surprise, saying that it seemed my career had flowed seamlessly and had only been filled with success. I said that is true, I've worked hard and been very lucky, there has indeed been success. Yet there have also been challenges and moments when I've questioned my path as well. Both things can be true at the same time. Derrick and I have both experienced this on the way to our Twenty One, you will as well.

At times it can be difficult to see a positive future in the midst of change. The reality is that life won't be the same afterward, it can't, but it is up to you to decide how it will be different. During life's inevitable changes you need to remember that you have more skills and opportunities than you imagine. Trust yourself and go for *The Crossover*.

Chapter Eight
One Step

I took a deep breath and realized that even though I didn't know exactly where I was going in life, I had to get moving, because if I didn't I was going to be in that little apartment in Madison, Wisconsin for a long time. It was time to start living my Twenty One Summers, which unbeknownst to me were going to take me places that twenty four year old me could not begin to imagine. This is a moment that I have lived in different variations throughout my life, and so have you. It is a time to reconsider, reboot, and evolve. It always comes down to the same decision, to take a breath, let go of pre-existing definitions and limitations, and begin moving forward, because the other choice is to stay exactly where you are, and that is not an option.

We all have moments in our lives, sometimes daily, when we need to make the decision to move forward or to stay stuck where we are. It can be something as simple as whether to get up and go to the store, or more substantial like ending a friendship, making a *Trade* and *Crossing Over* to a new career, or rededicating yourself to a healthier lifestyle. The list is as endless as everyone's Twenty One Summers combined. The first thing that you need to realize is that you have a choice, though it may not seem so at times, you do. You have the choice to live with peace, power, and clarity, to take control of your life. You also have the choice to let other people and everyday circumstances rule your life and make your decisions, to let the past decide who you will be in the future, or you can choose to completely give up. Don't let others or life's circumstances make that choice for you. All it takes is one small step to shift the story of your life in a positive way, and then a second one.

Twenty One Summers is about valuing your strengths, understanding and moving past your Blind Spots, working through your inhibitions, and making the decisions necessary to create the change you want to see in your life. By this point in the book you have defined the Blind Spots and habits that are keeping you from living the life you want to live. Your current set of Twenty One Summers should also be clear or at least coming into focus. The question is whether you have taken action, learned, tried something new, made a change, or are deciding how to take that first or second step. The goal is to live a more fulfilling life, however you define that. It is also about time. Better time management has numerous benefits as it will help you reduce stress while freeing up time to try new things as you work toward your Twenty One. Listen to that voice or feeling, the *Spark* inside of you that is urging you to action. The satisfaction of achieving something new and living a happier, peaceful, and more fully realized life is worth a little bit of your time. We will discuss time management later in this chapter. You will be surprised at how easy it is to find time for the things you want to do.

Whether you are facing a personal, emotional, financial, social, or professional challenge in life, change begins with the first step. The *Spark* for that step is an idea, emotion, realization, or longing that you feel inside that fills you with a desire or makes you uncomfortable in a way that you just cannot shake. It may also be the need to move ahead in the face of an inevitable or unexpected life change, whether that change is wanted or not. Once that *Spark* happens it can keep coming back letting you know that it is time for you to take action. That is when you take your first step.

That step can take shape in any number of ways. You might do some research regarding a topic online or in books and magazines, or you might begin by confiding with one of your family, friends, a local group, or your *Stars*. Another step might be to sign up for a class, a tutorial, or a consultation with someone you respect. As you do so, look for objective, helpful, information, and people who will support you as you change your life. Finding that support is essential. Remember that this is the beginning of your pathway, not the answer to all of your questions. Stay flexible and embrace the Agile and Iterative Processes along the way.

Throughout the book, we have seen first and second steps occur in a number of ways. Andrew Hawken who failed the 11 Plus exam was never a big reader and did not feel he was good at anything, yet he accepted the book *A Farewell to Arms* from his English teacher and took the time to read it cover to cover. It was not the choice that you would have expected. At that point, Andrew didn't have any idea what he was going to do in life but taking that first step changed everything. He began to read other authors and suddenly felt like, "OK, I can. I can do something." As we know that first step led to an extraordinary career.

Yves loved photography but didn't know that art school was an option. His high school didn't provide any depth in the arts, he didn't have people in his life who had creative careers, and he felt the weight of having to take care of his immediate family financially. The Blind Spots *Who Am I, Who Am I Supposed To Be* and *Who Can I Be* were hard at work. Yves's first step was to go out and photograph his neighborhood, despite not being able to afford to do so. The second was spending time looking at photography books in the school library while waiting for his mother to get home, instead of going out with friends. The third step was saying yes to the summer program at Wesleyan University, and the next was meeting regularly with Gordon Parks. Meetings that fed a desire to learn that Yves embraces to this day. If he hadn't taken those first steps and trusted the process, his life would be very different.

We first met Cira and Pasang in Chapter Two. Cira's *Spark* was a desire to take photographs. The first step was asking for a camera. The next was embracing her grandfather's old camera when her father took it off the shelf, giving Cira a lifetime of travel, photo and film making, and a venue for supporting women's dreams. Her parents did not believe that photography and adventure travel were appropriate for a girl, but a mix of desire and the strength to take *One Step* at a time has given Cira a life she could not have imagined. Pasang's willingness to go into the mountains and then to France to become Nepal's first female mountaineering instructor were enormous steps for her, ones that flew in the face of local belief systems. Doing so forever changed her life.

Pasang and Cira's story of empowerment resonates for many. It is one that asks *Who Am I Supposed To Be, Who Can I Be*, and *Yes, But Who Am I Really*, while questioning *Make Me Comfortable* and what that means in the context of the culture in which you live. Neither woman's family nor community felt their choices in life were appropriate for women and worked to discourage their efforts and dreams. Both women used those messages as motivation. Together, they developed an understanding that helped them move beyond the resistance they encountered and on to their next set of Twenty One, including Summers they could never have envisioned when they started.

Monica spent years debating whether she could or should go to grad school and restart her career. It had been difficult to get a good job after taking time off to raise her daughter and support her husband's return to school. She wanted to do something satisfying that would also help pay the bills, but time was passing her by. These were her *Sparks*. Her first step was to look into online grad schools to see what her options were. The second was to ask for the same time and respect at home that she had been giving her family for years. The third was applying to school, which turned out to be a longer process than she had imagined. Monica is now a licensed therapist with a full roster of clients. She is happier, more confident, and brings a new energy into their home. It was a lot of work, but she has slowly built a new life and lifestyle that has benefited everyone in her family.

There is not one answer to what your first step should be after you feel a *Spark*. As you can see from the stories in the book, there are many ways to approach a first or second step. You might build toward your first step and take it when you feel ready like Katya did when she booked her first tennis lesson, or perhaps there are a series of steps that lead you in the direction of your goals like we saw with Yves. Both ways are viable, just be sure not to let procrastination or your Blind Spots get in the way.

You don't need to be an expert or have enormous success right away. Simone Biles, Messi, and Anthony Bourdain all had to go through the Iterative Process. They pushed themselves to try new things, made mistakes, incorporated feedback, learned as they grew, and adjusted their goals as new opportunities and challenges presented themselves along the way. It is impossible to be Mikhail Baryshnikov the first time you dance or Miles Davis when you play your first song. Start by learning the basics and then take the steps necessary to get closer to your Twenty One. If you can't bring yourself to take the first step down the pathway then the rest of the path will forever stay closed. You have to do it. You simply have to. The transformation begins today.

If you are not sure which direction to go, start by writing down your biggest and smallest Summers. That might be buying your first house, downsizing where you live, or cleaning out your closet. Select one big Summer from your list and write down the steps that you imagine it will take to make that Summer come true. If you want to be a rock star, you might begin writing songs or practicing every day. If you would like to drive in the Indy 500, maybe you start by driving go-carts and move up the ladder to larger more powerful vehicles on the track. As we have seen, there are a number of pathways to your Twenty One, all begin with a series of small steps, each step building on the last.

Next, choose one or two smaller goals and make them happen simply because you can. Try baking cookies, they may not come out right the first couple of times, but it's all part of the process. Maybe clean out a kitchen drawer, take a few photographs, or go for a five minute walk in the morning. The list of small goals that you can reach is endless and the satisfaction of achieving them only strengthens your confidence.

Sometimes it's hard to define what you want, other times you know but you are afraid to admit it to yourself or others. The same goes for the choices you make in your everyday life. There are days that it is easy to admit what you desire and step up to the task, other times, all of your Blind Spots are working against you. We all have moments without clarity and times that we choose to ignore what we already know deep inside. The key is not to let those moments define you. Do not indulge in excuses; we know there always is one available if you need it but beginning today those excuses don't count. Keep the momentum going because that is how you change your life. Let those small steps blossom into your Twenty One Summers.

If you find it hard to step up to making bread, cleaning out your closet, or a larger task, ask yourself why. What is really holding you back? Talk to a *Star*, friend, family member, a health care professional, or a community group that you trust as you try to understand what your Blind Spot truly is. Perhaps deep down inside you know what is keeping you from moving forward but don't want to say it out loud. It could be personal, family, a cultural history, or an insecurity that only you know about. Admit the cause, at least to yourself, and then do the work to overcome it *One Step* at a time. Whatever your challenge, we know that coming to terms with it may not be easy, but the work you put in, the clarity you find, and the new life that you give yourself will be far better than feeling stuck or unhappy. Prove to yourself that you are stronger than the issue holding you back and remember, no excuses.

We often make taking that first step far more difficult than it really is. Imagine yourself standing in a warm room wearing a hat and coat while complaining about how hot you are. A friend listening to you complain suggests taking off the coat and hat, but you say no because you are concerned about what people will think about your hair or the clothes you are wearing underneath. Even though you know how to solve your problem, you are not willing to take a single step to make things better. It is a lot like life for some people. They can always find a reason to reject a solution. Stop complaining about how awful things are and take a step to improve your life. Sometimes it is as easy as taking off your coat.

This is a simple analogy but one that is so true. Though we feel discomfort, we often come up with reasons to embrace the status quo and complain when it would be far easier to take a step toward making life a bit better.

There are times when a Blind Spot isn't the only issue that you're facing; you may find that your life has changed while your goals have not. New desires often arise along with personal and professional challenges. Sometimes, those challenges are the gateway to where you truly need to be. Life may be giving you a nudge or perhaps testing you, trying to move you away from complacency and a way of viewing your life that has you stuck in place. Let go of *Make Me Comfortable*, look at potential *Trades*, consider *The Crossover*, check the *Walls of Your Knowledge*, and then review your Twenty One with fresh eyes. It is your life: own it, live it.

If you have just retired, take a moment and appreciate everything that you have accomplished in life. Know that an incredible and at times difficult chapter is closing and it is time for another. Remember everything that you did between the ages of ten and thirty one or twenty and forty one. You have at least the same amount of time available to you now, fill it beautifully. It may mean breaking up with the definition of yourself that you and others have had for a long time, and that is hard to do. It is hard to become "the former" whatever your job title was, but you need to do so to enable yourself to embrace the time ahead of you. If you have family and friends, enjoy them. If you like to travel and take pictures, do so, even if it is around your local community. Post your pictures online or join a local art space and exhibit your photographs. Why not? Join a local club, read books, play games. Volunteer and teach kids how to run a business. Start a new business focused on something you love and do it simply because you want to. Write the book that you've always wanted to write, go for long walks, work with a local not for profit to help children or elders, learn to ski, mountain climb, bike. Take a class and try that dance you have always wanted to learn. One day my parents said they were going to take up square dancing. They had enjoyed dancing in the living room when we were kids and I knew that they danced before they were married. Still, I thought they were crazy, but they had an amazing time. They made new friends, traveled, and it was great exercise.

You are the only thing getting in the way of a richer life. It is possible to change your perspective and allow yourself to try new and unexpected things. A big part of that is looking at *Who Am I, Who Am I Supposed To Be,* and *Who Can I Be.* Those Blind Spots apply at any age. Of course, we understand that circumstances may be harder for some of us than others but there are always options available to you. Come up with new Summers big and small. Let go of your old boundaries and inhibitions. Work through your Blind Spots and begin the process of making those Summers happen. You will be surprised at where life may take you.

Whatever stage of life that you are in, the initial drive to move forward must come from inside you. It will be up to you to take the first step and build new habits by integrating small changes on a consistent basis. Over time those new habits and ways of thinking will become easier for you. Like a new pair of shoes, they take time to get used to. Soon, they will be part of your life.

The key to building a habit is repetition. At first you may push back against change. If you find yourself doing so, take a breath and relax. Don't let yourself give in or give up, just take one more step, do one more repetition. Remind yourself that struggle is often part of growth. You may stumble at some point. Not to worry, we all have setbacks. Trust the process, it works. Keep pressing forward and believe in the power of you. Find your inner strength, you are the best ally that anyone could have.

At this point you may be saying that this all sounds good but wonder where you can find the time to add even the smallest Twenty One to your day. Whether you have just graduated, are mid-life and mid-career, or retiring, time management is essential.

Derrick developed a system for time management while working at Microsoft that will help you as you work toward your goals. Start by making a list of the time dedicated to your responsibilities and then list how you spend the rest of the day. Look at the list honestly and ask yourself where you can save ten minutes. Ten minutes a day equals sixty hours a year, or two a half days. Fifteen minutes a day is just over ninety one hours, or almost four days a year. That is between two and a half and four days to spend learning, growing, enjoying life, just by being a little more efficient. It is an incredible reward.

As you make your list, think of the time spent scrolling on your phone, distracted by news, looking at videos, staring at the TV, deciding what to wear, slow rolling through your morning or evening routine, or at long meals. Then ask yourself where you can be more efficient. At first glance you might not believe that there are ten extra minutes in your day, but there are. There will be *Trades* to make but we already know that.

It is easy to fill your time with little things that don't move your life forward or to let one or two chores fill your entire day. It is amazing to me how many people let one or two errands take up their entire schedule while others turn them into two quick stops. Being more efficient isn't difficult. Simple choices like being aware of how long it takes you to get out of the house or not planning one errand in the middle of the day will help. Schedule things together so that you make one trip instead of two, even if it means waiting a day to run one of your errands. A lot of readers will say, "Of course," but you would be surprised at how many people allow one task to fill hours.

Bad time management is also a way for some to avoid being accountable to themselves and their Twenty One. For some, avoidance seems easier than working toward positive change and a more fulfilling life. Consciously or subconsciously, time slowly slips by as hours become days, and days become weeks and years. Too many people never really take on the challenge of creating change in their lives. They let time pass and inertia sets in. I find that people who manage time badly frequently talk about how busy they are and the people I know who are the busiest at making life happen, whether that is work, personal growth, family, or play, rarely talk about how busy they are. They may complain a bit about a lack of time, but that is because they want to do more. They are people who love to learn, who have made their *Trades*, moved past *Make Me Comfortable*, are open to taking on *Who Am I Really*, and are on the pathway to their Twenty One.

If you find yourself stuck, ask yourself where your "I can'ts" are coming from. Check your Blind Spots to see which ones are at play. If necessary, redefine your goals and reset your Twenty One. Bad habits and Blind Spots will do their best to hold you back. Don't let them win; begin moving down the road to a happier and more efficient you.

In the end, time is all we have. You might say that we have family, friends, relationships, work, loves, hobbies, travel and so many more things that we value dearly. That is true, but the only way that we can enjoy these things is with time. As we know, there is less time in life than we imagine and Summers pass by quickly. The summers of our childhood seemed long and indulgent. As we get older, summers seem to become shorter and each day passes more rapidly, making it all the more important to value every one of them. So, begin to prioritize the things you love and those you want to achieve. Stop spending time in a slow drift through your day or a manic run from morning until night. Let life become richer and more fulfilling in big ways and small.

McKenzie and Tate are a couple in their late twenties. Together they enjoy and explore the beauty of the mountains in the American West. McKenzie is an oil painter.

Drawing inspiration from John Singer Sargent, she places skiers in vast mountain scenes during the winter, and in the spring and summer paints lush landscapes *en plein air* that reflect her deep appreciation for nature's beauty. Her paintings are in demand, as commissions and sales of existing works come in as fast as she can make them, which is admirable for a painter, as it can be a challenging field. Her husband Tate is in school working toward his PhD in Clinical Psychology and spends a large part of his time at school and studying. Together, they are bright, friendly, and conversational, their support for each other is moving.

As they were describing their career paths, Tate mentioned his admiration of McKenzie as in addition to her career, she also takes care of their two young children, finding time to paint early in the morning before they wake, during the day while they nap, and in the evening after they fall asleep. McKenzie smiled and said that it was a lot, but that she loves painting and that Tate will only be in school for a couple more years, after which he will be able to share the load more evenly. There was a light at the end of the tunnel.

I admired the way they talked about their lives, their support and appreciation for one another, and the peace with which they seem to navigate the demands they both face. As for McKenzie, she is truly someone who has found time within a more than busy life to focus on what she loves. She looks for those thirty minute blocks of time each day that add up to days of painting each year. Is it difficult? Without question, but she is an incredible example of someone who understands time and how a few minutes each day allows her to work toward her Twenty One

Summers. Sacrificing for her family while staying true to herself.

It is amazing what can be accomplished in fifteen minutes a day, thirty minutes three times a week, or a three hour workshop one day a month. All of your Blind Spots can shift. *Who Am I, Who Am I Supposed To Be, Who Can I Be, Make Me Comfortable, Yes, But Who Am I Really, Knowledge As A Wall, The Trade, The Crossover,* and *One Step,* can all be addressed by making a little time and taking action.

Derrick's system of time management is based on six principles that can help you save time. Following is a simplified version of the system used by many at Microsoft to help make themselves and the company more efficient.

Principle 1: Be ruthless with how you allocate your time

Principle 2: Allocate time to mandatory items first

Principle 3: Allocate your free time to your personal

priorities in order of importance

Principle 4: Be flexible as things change, but keep your

priorities clear

Principle 5: Continuously review

Principle 6: Maintain a long term and short view of time

Principle 1: Be ruthless with how you allocate your time

Ruthless may sound strong, but it is an appropriate word. If you don't set boundaries and manage your time, others will, or it will slip away one drop at a time until you wonder why the glass is half full when you haven't even taken a drink.

Time is one of the most valuable assets you have. Time is the future, it is your joys, your hopes, your challenges, your responsibilities, it allows everything that we want and have to do, it is your Twenty One, and luckily you can choose how you use it. It is very easy to get lost in your responsibilities and find yourself at the end of each day, week, or year wondering where all your time went. However, if you are ruthless with your time, you can maximize your free time and invest it in the things you want to do, not just the things you have to do. Then time won't slip away leaving you wondering what happened.

Principle 2: Allocate time to mandatory items first

You will always have necessities and responsibilities that take up a portion of your time. Sometimes they feel like they are taking up all of your time and energy, but that should not be the case. Before you can efficiently manage your obligations, you need to understand how much time they consume and where you can be more effective. Take a minute and make a list of your responsibilities and how much time they take each day. Then look for ways that you can reduce the time spent on each one. Slowly get your obligations under control, even if it is by a small amount.

Principle 3: Allocate your free time to your personal priorities in order of importance

Now that you have an idea of how much time you are spending on your obligations, it is essential to clarify your personal priorities. Begin with the list of your Twenty One and add new ideas to it, don't hold back. As you review your list, look at each item and decide its relative importance to you and your life. You will find that there are long term priorities that may take months or years to achieve and short term priorities that might take a few days, a week, or a month. Doing one or two push-ups and sit-ups a day to build strength would be a short term goal. A longer term goal would be becoming strong enough to hike up a local hill or do your first Ironman competition. Both types of goals are important.

Narrowing your list may not be easy and there will be some *Trades*, but it will force you to grapple with what is truly important. When in class I asked students to narrow their list to ten options, then to cross off three items, then two more, and finally two more, leaving their top three Summers. If you are going to spend your time wisely, you will need to prioritize. This will allow you to take care of your responsibilities as well as giving you time to do the things you truly want to do.

Principle 4: Be flexible as things change, but keep your priorities clear

Life is complex, every day brings new challenges and opportunities, some of which alter life in unimagined ways. New responsibilities will arise and *Trades* regarding your time and energy will have to be made. During times of change, strive to remain as flexible as possible. Utilize the Agile Process and adapt your plans as you move forward. As you do so be sure to keep your priorities clear.

It is easy to become consumed by change and lose sight of your goals. When you feel yourself doing so, slow down, take a breath, review how you are allocating your time, and if necessary adjust your Twenty One. Do not let chaos reign; take control of your life *One Step*, one decision at a time. Take care of your responsibilities and stay focused on keeping your free time yours. You deserve to achieve your Twenty One, even when life has other ideas.

Principle 5: Continuously review your time management

Time management is a skill that can be learned and improved over time. The key to improvement is to develop and refine an awareness of how you use your time and to review your performance regularly.

This review needs to be honest and objective. Did you use your time as you planned? Did you accomplish the goals you set? If not, what happened? Did old habits and Blind Spots pop up consuming valuable hours? How could you have managed your time better? If you want to do the things you love in life you must be aware of how and where you allocate your time and whether that allocation is helping you reach your goals. Then you need to make the choices necessary to keep yourself on track. Set boundaries as there will be times when people will question the time and commitment you dedicate to creating positive change. The need to stay strong and focused is obvious, if you let others sway you from doing the work necessary to improve your life, it will not happen.

Principle 6: Maintain a long term and short term view of time

When setting your priorities, it is important to balance long and short term perspectives as long term goals need to be mapped into short term time management. A New Year's resolution to be healthier at the end of three hundred and sixty five days is one thing but adjusting your schedule to eat better and exercise daily is a different challenge. Everything seems possible on day one, but your goals may be far more challenging when implemented on a day to day basis.

It may not be possible to use all of your free time as you wish but try your best to make each day worthwhile. Be aware of things that are neither your responsibility nor part of your Twenty One. Time that is spent listlessly, just passing you by. In your mind this may not be wasted time, but it is most likely time spent inefficiently, time that could be better used. Of course, we all need to relax, be sure to include that in your schedule too, but don't let it take all of your extra time or become an excuse for not taking action. If McKenzie can find a way to build a career painting with a husband at school and two children at home, you can certainly find a few minutes a day to improve your life and work toward your goals. It can be done.

Sometimes you need to be a little creative when it comes to saving time. That is when layering tasks will help. Let's say that it's Saturday afternoon and you have household chores to do, kids to watch, and you would like to spend time gardening. You might not be able to fit all three into the few hours that you have that day, but there are other options. Maybe you can do something with your children that is centered around gardening. That way you can spend time together as they experience something you love. Perhaps you have a friend who loves gardening as well. Invite your friend and their children over so you can both garden as your kids play nearby. If you are doing chores, your friend can help watch the kids while you work and the two of you catch up. These may seem like obvious and perhaps imperfect solutions but they each allow you to maximize your time while enjoying yourself. As you become better at time management you will begin to see new time saving options that may not be apparent to you now.

Once your priorities are set and your goals become more clearly defined it will be easier to say no to time consuming obligations. Setting those boundaries will give you more time for the people and things that are important to you and the lifestyle that you would like to live. Of course, be kind as you say no to demanding people, opportunities that may distract, and new responsibilities, but be straightforward as well. Do not feel like you need to apologize for focusing on the things that are important to you. You cannot do everything for everyone, that is impossible. If you try to do so others might be happy, but you won't. Remember, it is OK to take care of yourself. Setting boundaries, valuing your time, and the ability to say no are important steps toward realizing your Twenty One Summers and the life you desire.

As you make these choices consider the work/life balance we discussed in Chapter Six. Remember, there isn't a single answer to what that balance should be. Many experts will tell you what portion of your life should consist of work, play, or family, but those percentages may not apply to you. For you, work and play may be synonymous, meaning work or practice will take up more of your time. The same is true if you have financial or familial obligations demanding a greater portion of your time. In those instances, your work/life balance will adjust accordingly. In the end, the division of time and effort that comprises your work/life balance is entirely up to you. Strive to find a balance that is healthy and gives you the best chance to achieve your goals.

As we have noted, managing time in your professional life is important too and there are some rather easy solutions to doing so that may apply to your everyday life as well. Let's say that you run eight one hour meetings a day. Shortening each meeting by five minutes will give you forty extra minutes each day. Reducing each meeting by ten minutes will give you an hour and twenty minutes, which is a substantial amount of time to do the work you want or need to do. In the office this can easily be done by setting up and testing tech before the meeting starts, starting and wrapping on time, focusing on core topics, and asking for more focused and concise presentations.

There are other ways that you can create efficiencies throughout the day as well. Reed Krakoff used to say, "Let's walk" and we would have conversations while walking from our meeting to his next one. It was a simple way to use the time spent going from one place to another. It is a tool that I have used in my career and personal life, utilizing the time between meetings or while walking on the streets of New York. I often make personal and professional phone calls while driving or taking an Uber, using time that would otherwise be wasted. Take breaks and enjoy the ride, but also use some of that time to your advantage.

Another suggestion for managing your time is to open your calendar every six months and review the places you are spending large portions of your time, especially recurring commitments. Derrick used to do this at Microsoft, it gave him the opportunity to remove unnecessary meetings and obligations that had run their course. Whether at work or in your personal life, it is easy to get caught up in recurring obligations. By clearing your calendar and reorganizing, you give yourself the opportunity to reset your focus and take back your time.

Personally, I follow a similar set of principles to Derrick's Six, but in all honesty I have never been able to make a five year plan and rarely make plans for more than one or two years out, as I find it limits my options, implies a lack of personal growth over time, and assumes things will stay the same. At the least it would mean that I could predict life five years out, which has never been possible. Imagine trying to predict your senior year in high school while in eighth grade, your first year out of college when you are a senior in high school, or life five years after starting a new job or retiring. You can't do it. Our lives may become steadier and more predictable over time, but I have found that there are always surprises. I like my time horizon to be flexible as it allows me to visualize different outcomes or to embrace opportunities that I could not have imagined and then take the steps necessary to realize them.

That said, setting long term goals such as writing this book involves a multi-year timeframe. Better health and other personal and professional goals with a one or two year time horizon need to be set as well. Then, using the Agile Process, adjustments are made as unexpected life events arise or there are challenges within a project. For example, one chapter may take longer to write than planned which changes the overall timeline for the book and the amount of time that goes toward writing each day. Travel always presents challenges in terms of work and exercise, so *Trades* need to be made while on the road. These are nice issues to have, but it does mean adjusting my time and goals on a short term and long term basis. Finding time and having the discipline to work while traveling has always been difficult, but I understand that spending a day working when in a different city or country is what allows me to travel in the first place. So despite being somewhere that may be alluring, I carve out time to work. It is a very fair *Trade*, if at times a hard one.

Overall, I have become more ruthless regarding my time when it comes to eating better, working out, getting my work done, and spending time with the people I care about. There is always a reason not to take the next step or follow the guidelines I've set to reach my goals. Holidays come up and that means amazing food, friends and colleagues might want to meet for dinner, or my girlfriend and I may want to have pastries and coffee together just because we enjoy it. For years, I found myself giving in to all of those things for any number of reasons. Going out to eat was a big event while growing up, and we enjoyed it fully. It was a shared moment of family and celebration and that extended to how I viewed life and food as an adult. Also, part of me thought it rude not to indulge when going out. I didn't want to waste food, nor did I want to miss a special time with people that I cared about. There was always a list of reasons to ignore my personal goals, but in the long run that just didn't work.

Now that personal boundaries are set, I feel more comfortable cutting back and have found that nobody is offended. Everyone understands, particularly those closest to me. Setting priorities and sticking to them was a big step, one made up of a series of smaller steps that are allowing me to reach a number of my Core Twenty One. It can be a slow process at times, but I enjoy life and the people and places in it and want the quality of life to be as good as it can until the end of my time.

As you know, there are always distractions and responsibilities that can keep you from your goals. Like Derrick, I have always enjoyed what I do, though there have been times in life when I have had jobs or responsibilities that I didn't like or felt overwhelming. For instance, managing our apartment complex and running a business while in school, or taking a job in a movie theater so that I could stay in Los Angeles. When working long hours or taking jobs for the money or experience, I have reminded myself that these were *Trades* of time and effort that were necessary if I wanted to do the things I love. This meant reprioritizing time and adjusting short term goals to help reach longer term goals and my Twenty One. Learning discipline and making those short term sacrifices were necessary to change my life, career, and lifestyle. They were *Trades* that I was willing to make.

Once my priorities changed it became easier to let go of habits that were a waste of time. There are certainly days that I want to go back to my old ways of living, ways that are more lazy and less efficient. If I do, it doesn't take long for me to get back on course as I feel better living a life that has a greater sense of purpose and satisfaction. Whether that means achieving small daily goals that are only important to me or larger goals that are more visible and happen in a longer time frame.

To that end I check in on my time management daily, reviewing how my choices tie into short term, mid-term, and longer term goals. I do keep lists as they are helpful in terms of prioritizing goals and responsibilities, allowing me to focus on what needs to be done first. Short term priorities may always seem like they deserve attention, but longer term objectives need to be allocated time as well if they are going to be accomplished. The overarching goal is to work toward my Twenty One and continue to build the lifestyle that I want to live. When I get tired or begin to lose focus I remind myself that the difference between good and great is a thousand small steps and take the next one along the pathway.

Your Twenty One, how you prioritize time, and the steps you take, are often defined by your Core Values. When Derrick and I first discussed Core Values, we both admitted that we have never liked being asked "What are your Core Values?" and had historically had a difficult time answering the question. Yet as you design your life and choose your Twenty One, it is important to understand what your Core Values are, as they will give clarity to your choices and strength to your decisions. Many of your Core Values stay the same throughout your life, but as you work through *Who Can I Be, Yes, But Who Am I Really*, and expand the *Walls of Your Knowledge* some will inevitably evolve.

Personally, freedom is central to my Core Values, it is from there that other values grow. The freedom to create, the freedom to express opinions, the freedom to travel, to experience life, and to help others grow and succeed, are all part of my value system. Hard work, respect, and appreciation are Core Values that came from my family. They are based on respect for the work and care that my mother and father put in as they worked to give us all a good home and a better life. I don't know anyone who worked harder than my father, and he did so without complaint. I don't think that I will ever be able to match his hard work and dedication, but I strive to do things that would make him proud.

There is certainly more to my personal value system, but the values mentioned above have driven my life and career choices, the *Trades* made, the way time is managed, and the steps that I have taken along the way. Sometimes they influence my decisions consciously and other times subconsciously. There were times when I could not identify or explain my Core Values, times when my Blind Spots were overwhelming and I wasn't sure what the answer was or the next step to take. Yet like that morning in my apartment in Madison I knew that steps had to be taken, and they were. Slowly moving forward along the pathway to where I am today.

At this point in his life, Derrick's Core Values are independence and fairness. He too has a broader value system, but these are the Core Values that drive him. Independence is his primary value, the one the others are based on. He feels the most at peace when he is able to act independently, which manifests itself in ways both good and bad. On the positive side it allows him to be self-motivated, curious, willing to take risks, gives him the ability to follow his dreams, and makes him personally accountable for his choices. As a leader this Core Value was helpful, as he was comfortable being out in front of a project, taking responsibility and leading the team.

However, there is a negative side to being independent as well. In general, it means that Derrick can find it challenging to be a great team player at work or in sports. The sports side of things is relatively easy, as Derrick prefers solo sports such as snowboarding or mountain biking that can be done individually. At work, his vision and independence made him a valuable asset. It also meant that he expected his teammates to follow his pace and keep up. As we learned in Chapter Three, this worked well when he was in a senior role, managing people who were experienced and equally driven, but in his earlier years with Microsoft he found himself disguising his most important Core Value, the one that ultimately led to his success. It wasn't until one of his *Mentors* made him aware of how his independence was affecting his team and colleagues around him that he understood the issue this Core Value was creating. To his credit, he then strove to find balance between one of his greatest strengths and the ways in which it could be a weakness in a business context. Derrick's second Core Value is fairness. He often thought about becoming a lawyer but realized early on that he wouldn't enjoy practicing law as it is too rule based, putting it in conflict with his primary Core Value, independence. For him, the spirit of the law is finding a fair outcome for everyone involved. It is his nature.

Whether at work or in his personal life Derrick has learned that others won't always share his values. When facing these situations, he has found the best response is to explain the rationale behind his choices. Though he isn't one hundred percent successful, taking the time to explain his thought process allows him to manifest his Core Values and hopefully make life fairer for others.

Your Core Values will influence how you spend your time and define your Twenty One. They will help you clarify your goals and understand the next steps going forward. Just like your Summers these values can and should evolve, and like your Blind Spots they will drive your decision making, oftentimes without your knowing it. Spend a few minutes and write down your Core Values. See if they align with your life choices, time management, and Twenty One. Like Derrick and me, you may find it difficult to identify your Core Values. If so, start with a list of the things that you value in life. Do not censor yourself or let *Who Can I Be, Who Am I Supposed To Be, Who Can I Be, Yes, But Who Am I Really*, or *Make Me Comfortable*, define your values for you. Make sure that they are your own and not values that others have set for you.

When you find yourself struggling to move forward, look for that first step and take it, whether it is big or small. Stay focused. Don't let others dismiss your dreams or harsh critique keep you from doing the things you need or love. It is important not to let others tell you what to dream in life, whether that is an individual person, family, teacher, community, social media, TikTok, YouTube, celebrities, or a group that you belong to. Look to yourself for validation, placing your personal happiness and achievements ahead of accolades from others. Too many people live others' dreams or talk their future out of existence before they even begin. Don't compare your Twenty One with other people's Summers. Your Twenty One are filled with your own beautiful goals and desires. Cherish them, let them evolve, and most of all make them your own. This is no longer a list, it is your life. Take the first steps toward changing your life into the one you deserve and desire.

Chapter Nine
Designing Your Life

Throughout the book we have talked about the value of time and the processes that you can follow to make your life more fulfilling. You know that you have the power to effect change and the ability to take the first steps into a new life whether that is after graduating from school, adjusting to mid-life change, moving into retirement, or working to make every day a little brighter for yourself or others. We have discussed letting go of the preconceptions and definitions that hold you back as you take steps toward your goals. With each chapter we have provided stories, insights, and inspirations that, along with doing the unavoidable work, can provide a pathway toward growth and change.

By now writing an ever evolving list of your Twenty One, taking on Blind Spots, expanding the *Walls of Your Knowledge*, making *Trades*, managing your time, and taking the steps necessary to move your life forward, should be part of your personal process. At the least you should be laying the groundwork to take that first step toward growth, change, or something you have been yearning to learn or experience.

As you work toward your Twenty One Summers, imagine yourself *Designing Your Life*. Each step, each of your Twenty One bringing you closer to living a lifestyle that you desire and deserve. A lifestyle defined by your Core

Values, beliefs, and the things that ultimately make you happy. *Designing Your Life* doesn't mean living a predefined plan, just like your Twenty One Summers are not made up of immovable goals. As you know, the life that you design and the Summers that comprise it will evolve along the way. The decisions you make as you take on *Who Am I, Who Am I Supposed To Be, Who Can I Be*, move past *Make Me Comfortable*, and resolve *Yes, But Who Am I Really*, will help define the lifestyle that you create, as will all of your *Trades* and *Crossovers* and how you move past the *Walls of Your Knowledge*.

When you choose a career, relationship, hobby, work through a Blind Spot, or address a change in life, think about more than that decision alone, also consider the lifestyle that choice will bring. As you learned when studying your Blind Spots, each city, state, or country you live in will largely dictate the lifestyle that you live. Every region has a way of life defined by local belief systems, community, geography, government, predominant businesses and industries, and cultural and educational institutions. Other variables such as what people do in their free time matters as well. Do they hike, go to the beach, surf, swim, ski, fish, hunt, paint, read a lot, like racing or vintage cars, attend the theater, get together at each other's homes, hang out at bars, spend time at cultural institutions? Do people in the area have a college, high school, post-college education, what kind of food do they eat, are they conservative or liberal, do they love sports, is there diversity of thought, and is good conversation embraced or not? These are just a few of the things that you should ask when looking for a place to live, work, or play. They are important parts of *Designing Your Life* and will influence your ability to achieve your Twenty One.

If you want to be a fashion designer or fashion photographer it may be hard to do so in Omaha, Nebraska, due to a lack of fashion brands, no national and international media outlets, and a less diverse range of personal style than you might find in Tokyo or New York. Being a fashion designer or photographer in Los Angeles or Miami may mean creating or photographing swimwear or athletic wear, with New York or Paris providing opportunities to work in high fashion or couture. Your goals might be the same in any of these cities, but the geography, lifestyle, people you collaborate with, cultural perspective, and businesses in the region, will change the type of work that you can do, and hence your lifestyle. If you love the ocean and spending time on big sandy beaches then taking a job in Salt Lake City, Utah might not be a good fit, but it would be perfect if you enjoyed hiking and skiing. If you want to be a country music singer or musician you will probably have to be in Nashville, Tennessee at some point in your career. In the end, your lifestyle will be defined in large part by where you are and the people and opportunities you surround yourself with.

Of course, there are times when you need to make lifestyle *Trades* for your job or relationship. Everyone that we have talked about in the book has done so in order to achieve their Twenty One. Each *Trade* was a step along the way to a larger goal. An example of this would be returning to school to learn a trade or earn a degree. Going back to school may not be the lifestyle you desire for the next two or four years, but it will give you the opportunity to reach your desired lifestyle after graduation. The time will pass either way and it is better to have learned a new skill. Another example might be taking a starter job that will allow you to transition into the position you want to have in the future. Your first job will probably not provide the ideal lifestyle, but it can be a step toward the life that you envision. These steps are necessary as we move through life. Just stay aware and do not let *Who Can I Be* or *Make Me Comfortable* take over. Once you settle into a way of living it can be easy for a few months to become a few years and a few years to become ten or twenty. If you don't keep moving forward one day you may wake up wondering how you ended up where you are.

Your relationships are some of the most important, rewarding, and at times difficult, aspects of your life. This is true whether we are talking about communities, friendships, colleagues at work, or personal relationships. The people that you invite into your daily interactions, whether colleagues, friends, or lovers, can have a profound effect on how you live. People often overlook the importance of lifestyle when thinking about a good friend, marriage, or moving in together and sharing your lives and home. We rarely consider the fact that we are marrying or moving in with a lifestyle in addition to a person. The lifestyle that you live together will be central to your happiness and the opportunities and challenges that will present themselves in life.

One evening, Derrick had a few friends over and decided to ask each person to name three of their Twenty One Summers and describe the lifestyle they wanted to live. The answers were eye opening to one couple who had been seeing each other for a few months. They enjoyed each other's company but found their personal drive, their *Spark*, and personal goals were extremely different. One was regularly asking *Who Can I Be* as they moved past *Make Me Comfortable*, while the other was complacent and had not really considered the question. It was an important conversation to have as their lifestyles will become a key part of their relationship.

Expanding your circle of friends and acquaintances can be a very healthy choice. When doing so don't just look for people exactly like you; consider what you will learn from those you meet, the lifestyle they live and whether they will support your goals and lifestyle choices. You are giving up valuable time when you bring someone new into your life. You are also introducing their lifestyle, healthy or unhealthy, into your days. Before taking the next step, ask yourself if you can manifest who you are and what you love in the business, community, relationship, or friendship you are thinking about being part of. It isn't always easy to say no to an unhealthy friendship, work environment, group of friends, or relationship, but as we have learned doing so is essential to moving forward in your life, living the lifestyle you want to live, and becoming who you want to be.

Hopefully we all evolve as we move through relationships and learn about ourselves, our strengths and weaknesses, and our needs, becoming better friends and partners along the way. Being honest with yourself about your Twenty One and aware of the lifestyle you and a potential partner each desire will help you make better choices and save you both challenges along the way. Things happen and relationships begin and end as you grow and life changes. That is the nature of things, but finding someone who understands your lifestyle and work/life balance will help you avoid potentially toxic situations and save yourself and others heartache and other issues along the way.

It can be difficult to stay objective when considering how a partner will affect your future lifestyle, particularly when you are in a potential long term relationship. This may be especially true if you have just left another relationship or it has been a while since you have had someone in your life. Feelings run strong and it can be hard to think clearly. Always ask yourself if the person you want to invite into your daily life will respect you, treat you well, share the load, be your biggest supporter, and truly help you advance your personal, professional, and emotional goals. This is the minimum we should expect from those we share our lives with. Do they live a lifestyle that you want to share, embrace, and make part of your world on a daily basis? To put it simply, is this person and their lifestyle additive or do they subtract from your time, effort, energy, and happiness? Can you fully be who you are and do what you love in this relationship? Will their lifestyle help you achieve your Twenty One or will you end up in conflict, perhaps living someone else's Summers? Though it may be hard to wait, it is better to enter a relationship when you are feeling strong, focused, and clear about yourself and your goals as opposed to coming from a place where you are feeling weak or unsure about yourself. That will allow you to make more objective decisions about who you bring into your life and how they will affect the way you live.

You may think that toxic environments are rare, but there are acquaintances, friends, lovers, family members, colleagues, and communities that will work to undermine your confidence and keep you from being happy or successful. As we discussed in Chapter Three, in these situations the pressure to conform may come through compliments, bullying, threats, being given rewards or having them withheld, alienation from a social group or committees and events within your organization, being given less desirable projects, or a number of other processes that may manipulate or coerce you into conforming to toxic methods of engagement and an unhealthy environment. Some people will want you to do less at work or in your personal life as it makes them feel more comfortable about their place in life, their beliefs, power, or success. Their goal may be twofold as it will help ensure their happiness and success at the cost of your own.

You will meet people who thrive by creating toxicity and chaos, engaging with the world in a manner that will only diminish others and their ability to realize their potential. Let that knowledge motivate you to take the first steps away from toxic individuals, organizations, and negative forms of conformity. As you *Design Your Life,* think about the lifestyle that you want to live and whether your relationship choices are helping you achieve your goals along the way.

In Chapter Seven, we saw a lifestyle choice play an important role in Hugh Williams's life and that of his family. One day he and his wife were hiking in the California hills talking about their lives and realized it was time to leave the US and move back home to Australia. Hugh had had an amazing run at Google, eBay, Tinder, Microsoft, and DoorDash, but they longed for the life and lifestyle of their former home. If you remember, the move also allowed Hugh and his wife to start what has become a very successful not for profit that has benefited hundreds of schools and tens of thousands of students in the country. The new opportunities brought by the move has changed Hugh's lifestyle and substantially altered the potential future for thousands of students as well.

Andrew Hawken failed the 11 Plus test when he was a child but went on to work at the BBC and Microsoft among other companies. Despite Andrew's success at Microsoft, his family wasn't happy in Seattle and wanted to move back to the UK, which meant a substantial *Trade* for Andrew. They longed for their life back in London, so Andrew regularly flew between the UK and Seattle. In the end commuting between two cities wasn't the lifestyle that he had hoped, so he left Microsoft and took a job running Sky News in London. It was a lifestyle change that, like Hugh's, led to a new opportunity.

As we know, running Sky News wasn't the last job Andrew would hold. While at Sky he saw the potential in virtual reality and decided to take time away from his job to explore possible business opportunities. Within a week he and his co-founder had launched Mesmerise, a company originally focused on virtual reality, now working in AI. The desire for a different lifestyle led him and his family back to England, but the change also opened up new possibilities. For Hugh and Andrew, success wasn't what ultimately made the difference in terms of whether they stayed in the States or moved back home, lifestyle was.

Kodo, the student who wanted to be a make-up artist and a monk, made a series of decisions based on the lifestyle that he wanted to live. When he left his home in Japan to move to New York, Kodo was able to embrace a city that allowed him to live an open lifestyle, one that was not available when he was younger. He later left New York to become a Buddhist monk. The longing to learn more about his family's Buddhist history and expand the *Walls of His Knowledge* took him to a monastery where he once again lived an entirely different life. As he studied, the increasing dissonance between his personal beliefs and the practices at the Temple led him to request a meeting with the Master of the Temple. Nervously, Kodo asked whether becoming a monk would mean disavowing his lifestyle, to which the Master answered that the most important message of their denomination is to tell everybody that we can all be equally loved. With consent from the Master of the Temple, Kodo understood that he could combine his two lifestyles and become an activist for acceptance and understanding. It was at this moment he realized that he needed to dedicate his life to helping others find the acceptance, freedom, and fortitude to be who they truly want to be. Kodo's ever evolving lifestyle goals have allowed him to reach many of his own Twenty One, while having experiences he never could have imagined when we first met.

The desire for change begins in many ways. We know that some life changes are thrust upon us and it is up to us to respond, taking the steps needed to lead us down a new path. Graduation or retirement are examples of inevitable changes that we can plan for but will never really understand until the time comes. Other changes come from a *Spark* or desire deep inside. Listen to that voice or feeling, that *Spark* inside of you that is urging you to action. It may be pressing you to overcome a barrier in life, to try something new, to become a stronger version of yourself, or take the first step toward building a new personal life or career. Each moment of change in life will either propel you forward or hold you back, the choice is yours. In the end they are all opportunities for positive change.

Challenges manifest themselves in each of our lives in different ways. You read about Cira and Pasang who both faced situations in which they were told "no" when it came to following their dreams as young women. Though from completely different cultures, they each needed to be strong enough to move past local bias to fulfill their personal and professional dreams. Together they took on the challenges of the mountains and gave each other the support necessary to keep going as new barriers arose in their lives.

Are you willing and able to identify the Blind Spots that are holding you back, distinguish ways to expand the *Walls of Your Knowledge*, pinpoint the *Trades* and *Crossovers* needed, and take the first step toward positive change and your potential future, or will you give in to challenging moments and let life and others make the decisions for you? If you have read this far, you are someone who believes they can effect change in their life and has a sense of the lifestyle they would like to live. You have the ability to identify your Twenty One and the power to begin achieving them.

There are times when accepting good things in life can be as difficult as overcoming challenges. Your Blind Spots can hinder your success, happiness, and fulfillment, often revealing themselves by undermining the good things that come your way. Sometimes it is a fear of success that keeps you from being happy or achieving your goals. We can be very sophisticated self-deceivers, telling ourselves that we are working toward our Twenty One when we are really coming up with all sorts of ways to keep them from happening. You know that excuses, reasons, and rationalizations are debilitating and do not have a place in your life. They keep you from believing in yourself and taking the next step forward. Let your thoughts roam widely, imagine things that are beyond your boundaries, and do not talk your dreams out of existence before you even begin. Embrace the moments when things are going well in life as opposed to pushing them away. As we have said many times, you deserve good things in life. You really do.

When looking at the life and career of Reed Krakoff, you might ask yourself if he has *Designed His Life*. I have never asked, but he has certainly been intentional in his choices, using the Agile Process to respond to change as he developed his skill sets, management style, creative vision, and the way he handled challenges and success. He has done so while combining his talents with his loves and interests to build a life that he truly enjoys. Reed has allowed himself to embrace the opportunities life brings while creating his own as well. Whether as a fashion designer, creative director, photographer, art and design collector, or creating books, he has surrounded himself with a strong team that he trusts and can believe in. That alone is a talent. One that has helped him reach many of his Twenty One.

Billy had a career that led him around the world. His life was filled with adventure that kept him sharp physically and mentally. Over the course of his service he lived simply, saved well, and was able to retire early. During lunch one day I asked him what he was going to do now that he had retired and he responded, "I hope this doesn't sound egotistical, but I'm going to focus on myself." He went on to explain that he wanted to continue to live simply and spend his time working out and expanding the *Walls of His Knowledge*. Every day he exercises, runs, and uses a device called The Bullworker. He has watched too many people allow themselves to slowly deteriorate physically and mentally and understands the challenges that can bring. That is a manifestation of his Core Values and it is his Core Summer. He is *Designing a Life* that will allow him to enjoy his time here and embrace many more Summers as he stays physically and mentally fit.

As we first mentioned in Chapter Six and again in Chapter Nine, each of the decisions you make includes a time component. Whether we are talking about the Summers of your teens and twenties, the Twenty One in your forties and fifties, or those after retirement, the way that you decide to spend your time is at the crux of Twenty One Summers. The only way to maximize time is to streamline life, giving you the time to focus on the things that are important to you, the Twenty One that bring you joy and fulfillment. It is up to you to decide what those are. Billy allocates his time in a way that allows him to work toward his core Twenty One. For Monica in Chapter One it was creating time in her busy family life to go back to school to get her master's degree online and become a therapist. Mark, the documentary photographer who we met in Chapter Seven, made the change from working photographer to a Senior Photo Editor at the New York Daily News. Then, exhausted by the intensity of the job he decided to move to Santa Fe, New Mexico where he rested and recuperated, detoxing from the demands of his work. Mark considered going back to work as a photographer, but the joy that had accompanied image making was missing. It was then that he decided to become an Emergency Medical Technician (EMT). He had always been hard working, compassionate, and driven to help others. His stories as a photographer and editor sought to bring understanding to the world and ultimately a positive message. Helping others as an EMT gave him the opportunity to put those traits to use daily, benefiting those he came in contact with and providing a deep sense of personal satisfaction. By reallocating his time and using *The Crossover* he was able to embrace his Core Values and create an opportunity that changed his life.

As you refine your Twenty One remember the six principles of time management; be ruthless with how you allocate your time, allocate time to mandatory items first, allocate your free time to your personal priorities in order of importance, be flexible as things change but keep your priorities clear and continuously review and maintain a long term and short view of time. Find the places in your day that you can save time, time that will add up to hours, days, weeks, or months. Apply that precious time to your Twenty One and enjoy a more satisfying life. In doing so create a work/life balance that fits your responsibilities and the lifestyle you aspire to.

The work/life balance that you end up with is entirely up to you. What that balance is will depend on your goals and responsibilities. At this point, we know that if you want to be Yayoi Kusama, Carrie Underwood, Warren Buffet, or Giannis Antetokounmpo, and do what you love for a living, you will need to devote a large portion of your time to learning and practice to achieve your goal. Though work and play may become synonymous, your work/life balance will lean dramatically toward your Core Summer, so there will be less time for other things in your life. That is one of the *Trades* that you have to make if you strive to achieve greatness. The difference between good and great is a thousand little things and it takes time and effort to get them right.

Greatness certainly doesn't need to be your goal. Many of us do not have the time or honestly the talent to achieve that level of success, and that is OK. Your goals may be very different, perhaps they are comprised of necessities such as children to take care of, medical bills to pay, a house that needs repair, or other demands on your time and resources. These are essential goals and responsibilities that deserve our time and effort. In these instances, your work/life balance will need to adjust accordingly. Try to find a balance that is healthy and gives you the best chance to achieve your Twenty One, whatever they are.

Being in a relationship, working with a colleague, or going through retirement with someone who is extraordinarily driven to achieve can be demanding. If you have someone like this in your life, their work, practice schedule, diet, or absolute focus on a specific goal or goals may be consuming and that can be difficult. If you are a person who is driven to explore or succeed it is essential to find someone who is comfortable with your lifestyle choice and the way of living that it brings.

Jimmy Chin is a professional mountain athlete, National Geographic photographer, Academy Award winning film director, and New York Times bestselling author. He has spent years in mountains, and more recently oceans, around the world. He began his career as a dirtbag climber in Yosemite, living out of his car for years, making just enough to get by and keep climbing while photographing his friends. He went on to become the world's premier adventure photographer and filmmaker. Jimmy and his wife, the award winning documentary film maker Elizabeth Chai Vasarhelyi, collaborated on their first movie together, *Free Solo*. The film documented Alex Honnold's journey to become the first person to climb the face of Yosemite's El Capitan without a rope. Scaling the face of El Capitan was a stunning achievement, as was the photographing and filming of Honnold's talent, dedication, and struggle to attain his goal. This was Chin and Vasarhelyi's first major project together and just one of many achievements in Honnold's extraordinary career as a climber and founder of the Honnold Foundation an environmental not for profit.

This brings us back to lifestyle and finding people who understand your devotion to something. Whether we are talking about Jimmy Chin and Elizabeth Chai Vasarhelyi, Alex Honnold and his wife Sanni McCandless, or you and your partner, finding someone who is able to understand and accept the sacrifice necessary for you to live the lifestyle you desire is essential. The same applies to the community you surround yourself with. Find people who understand and support you, your lifestyle, your happiness, and your Twenty One. Depending on where you live and what your lifestyle is that may be easier said than done but be patient as you find your community or they find you.

During Derrick's time at Microsoft he collaborated with and managed a number of very talented people. Surprisingly, many became stuck during their career unable to move past the level of success they had attained despite a desire to do so. The knowledge and skills that helped them achieve an advanced level of success were not the skills that were going to take them to the next level. Despite input from managers and *Mentors* many were not open to trying a different approach or changing their perspective. One or more of their Blind Spots was inhibiting their progress. In the end, the decision not to move past *Make Me Comfortable* and *Who Can I Be* and embrace *Knowledge As A Wall* placed a ceiling on their personal and professional growth. A ceiling that they each chose to create by refusing to engage in the Agile Process and refine their skills. We do this in many areas of our lives, it is what Blind Spots do, they hold us back often without our knowing. That is why it is imperative to be aware of your choices. You need to be conscious of the things that are holding you back and the potential challenges or roadblocks in the way of reaching your current Twenty One.

People who achieve at a high level often find it challenging to retire with many going back to work again before finally deciding it is time to move into the next phase of their lives. Many people in creative fields never retire. There are times when that is due to financial challenges, but more often it is because they cannot live without the stimulation and satisfaction that comes from creating. On the business side, Derrick and I both know people who have had extraordinary careers but cannot figure out what to do after retirement. A number of Derrick's colleagues have the intelligence and financial wherewithal to do whatever they wish but struggle to create their Twenty One after they leave work. It can be difficult to decide what is next, despite past success. As we mentioned above, the very things that made you successful can hold you back. There are a couple of reasons for this. First, we hold onto past successes because they are validating and feel good. That can be hard to walk away from. Second, we begin to believe that there is only one way to be successful and embrace the skills or lifestyle that have worked for us so far. You have to let go of *Make Me Comfortable* and allow yourself to evolve if you want to continue moving forward in life. The pathway toward your Twenty One is there if you are willing to take it.

While writing this book, a friend asked if Twenty One Summers applied if everything was going well in life. She explained that she was going to be closing what had been a successful company and wondered what she would do with her time now that a commitment volunteering for a not for profit was also coming to an end. We went on to discuss what her next step might be. Her life was full and things were indeed good, but the same questions arose for her as they have for Derrick's colleagues at work. What is next? How do I find it? Will it be fulfilling? We all reach these moments at some point in life when we find our Blind Spots working against us, even if things are going well. At that moment, you can dig deep and do the necessary work or give in and let life and others make the decision for you. Ultimately, the decision is yours. That is when taking the next step, staying the course, and trusting the process, becomes even more important.

My career has been defined by its evolution. Whether going back to school to get degrees that allowed me to move past the *Walls of My Knowledge*, engaging in the Iterative Process as an image maker, writer, speaker and educator, regularly examining *Who Am I*, *Who Am I Supposed To Be*, *Who Can I Be*, and *Yes, But Who Am I Really* while trying to understand life's possibilities, or moving past *Make Me Comfortable* while embracing new experiences, the ability to grow and change has been central to my life and work. Finding or developing relationships and communities that have supported this exploration has been essential to the process. It is not possible to reach your goals alone. Positive communities, friends, family, and *Stars* have been an important part of the mix, along with staying agile and aware.

As you might imagine, an important part of my process is regularly updating my Twenty One as I learn the limits of a skill set or business model, realize the potential in a newly discovered area of interest, become aware of a Blind Spot, or uncover new opportunities and the threads leading to possible futures. As you have read, challenges such as a double pulmonary embolism on a flight from China to Newark and the cancellation of a new business teaching workshops internationally have also played an important role in the evolution of my life and career. There have, of course, been wonderful gifts and opportunities as well. In a way, life has been a series of beautiful mistakes and happy accidents framed by good luck, gratitude, hard work, dedication, faith, and preparation. Putting in the time to make things happen is an unavoidable necessity. Even the smallest of your Twenty One requires making adjustments to how you manage your time and having the drive to make it happen.

There have been numerous personal and professional challenges, failures, and mistakes as well, some within my control and others outside of it. At each turn it was my job to reevaluate, learn, adjust, and evolve along the way. Taking the steps necessary to move forward and to find or build the threads to potential futures and the opportunities they might hold. The goal was a lifestyle, the ability to create, travel, and help others. Also to stay in good health and enjoy life until its end, embracing every possible Summer that I can along the way.

Derrick's career has evolved as well. Though he worked at a single company for the majority of his career the context in which he worked shifted as the corporation grew and his career progressed. He and his wife made the *Trade* to move from London to the United States and he dedicated the time necessary to achieve his career goals. Derrick chose to *Crossover* from engineering to marketing and back as he worked to expand the *Walls of His Knowledge* in ways that enabled him to have seven US Patents approved and nine US Patents pending, including one with Bill Gates. He has worked with partners such as Apple, Amazon, Meta, Twitter, and Yahoo, and on Microsoft products like Bing, Windows, Office Suite, Azure, Xbox, and AI. His growth as an innovator and manager was essential to his career. As you now know, he learned and grew from mistakes, failure, and success, following input from his *Mentors* and adjusting his approach along the way. He has embraced the possibilities that have come his way, living each of his Summers to their fullest. That has indeed been one of life's beautiful gifts.

Equally important, he believes that things will work out in life, a belief that we both hold, whether that is a personal project, a project at work, or one of his Summers. He understands that the worst thing that can happen is that he will fail and learn something from it or realize that what he attempted isn't one of his strengths and his time is better spent elsewhere. In the end both are positive results. This attitude is a large part of his success. When you trust the process, do the work, and begin to believe that things will work out, they usually will.

The people that we have introduced you to in the book have found success and happiness in a range of ways. Each of them has made brave decisions, just as you will. Though everyone has had their own Twenty One, their processes are comparable. It began with a *Spark* that they embraced, a *Spark* that led them down a path to new opportunities and the challenges that came along with them. Once a challenge or opportunity was identified they pushed past *Make Me Comfortable* and expanded the *Walls of Their Knowledge* as they redefined *Who Am I, Who Can I Be*, and *Yes, But Who Am I Really* while identifying solutions and looking for advice and support from the people and communities they trusted. They managed their time and developed a work/life balance that allowed them to succeed, each in their own way. In doing so, they have all changed their lives and the lives of those around them, building a lifestyle they desired in the process. You can do the same. As you look back through their stories you will see that though their pathways have been different everyone's process has been similar. This applies to Derrick and me as well. There is not a single path to your Twenty One and your definition of happiness, satisfaction, growth, or success, there are many.

The process that we have described in the book will help you find your path and navigate it. Of course there will be doubts along the way, that is natural, do not let them deter you. Doubts are a sign that you need to take a breath, refocus, review your Blind Spots, redefine your Twenty One, and then take a step forward. Slowly put your doubts behind you as you focus on what is next. Let yourself be inspired by the stories that you have read and the diverse range of lives and challenges they represent. As we have said, dreams are rarely achieved without opposition, but that is part of the satisfaction of making them come true. Trust yourself. That may take some time but trust yourself to be able to do the work you need to do. Know that you have the ability to reach your goals if you truly want to.

Make sure that those goals are yours: don't let others tell you what to dream of in life or what your lifestyle should be, not social media, YouTube, advertisements, celebrities, family, friends, teachers, or communities. Those are other people's limitations, aspirations, and ambitions. Steer clear of comparing your Twenty One with others and competing against them. That is a distraction in terms of your time and energy that will hold you back. You are only competing against yourself. Your dreams and your Twenty One are your own beautiful goals and desires. Cherish them, let them evolve, and most of all make them your own.

We know that taking that first step can be intimidating at times, but what if it's easier than you think? There are always things on my to do list that I agonize over. Then when I finally step up and get one of them done it is much easier and takes far less time than I imagined. In the end I wonder why I waited so long. Personally, it was a big step to get on a plane and go to Paris Fashion Week right after graduating from The Art Center College of Design. I was overwhelmed by the idea. Walking through the streets of Moscow and trying to set up meetings with artists and museums was intimidating as well. Not really knowing the language or how to get around made the decision to go to both cities daunting, but you take those first steps. Not because you know where they will lead, but because they are the doorway to new futures and unimagined possibilities.

As the book wraps up, I find myself thinking about the days and weeks after the embolism on a flight back to the United States from China, and the reasons for sharing that story with you, time, choice, effort, and gratitude. Time, because our time here is limited. I have always appreciated life and all that it brings but perhaps a bit more now as every additional moment seems a gift, one to be used to its greatest advantage. Choice, because the choice to stay and continue my work was one of the most powerful realizations from the experience. It is a decision that inspires and empowers me daily. We make choices like that throughout our lives, whether it is to love or support someone, to treat ourselves and others better, work toward living our dreams, devote ourselves to the effort and discipline it takes to reach goals large and small, or to enjoy the beauty of the good people around us and the magic of the day. Effort, because of the effort it took to rebuild my health and career, neither of which seemed guaranteed at the time. Also, the effort of those around me who continue to inspire by building extraordinary lives, taking on new challenges and growing daily, being good people, and helping others along the way. Gratitude, because now it permeates most everything that I do on some level. I have always been thankful for many things in life and still am, but lately I experience greater gratitude for an ever evolving Twenty One that challenges me daily. Life indeed continues to surprise.

Now it's time for you to walk onto your own stage, whether that is in the privacy of your home, at work, with one of your friends or *Stars*, in your local community, or around the world. As you survey your life and begin to make choices ask yourself what and why. Just like my students at the beginning of the semester asking themselves why they were at that school, sitting in that class, and studying for that degree, you need to ask yourself why you are where you are in life and what you truly want to do next. If you've just graduated, don't get stuck in your apartment, take the first step along what has the potential to be an incredible path. If you're mid-life and facing a challenge, wondering about a change, or unhappy with where you are, begin to make a list of your Twenty One and break down the Blind Spots that are holding you back. If you're retiring, do the same. Life is giving you a fresh start and more time, our most valuable asset. Take hold of the agency and power that you have over your life. If you're waiting for permission, you have it. Go for it.

As you layout your Twenty One, be sure to identify your Core Values and desires. Don't be afraid of them, embrace them and make them yours. Define and work through your Blind Spots, they will always be with you, but you will find they become less prevalent with time and effort. Expand the *Walls of Your Knowledge* and surround yourself with *Teachers, Mentors, Pillars*, and others who will support you as you build a positive environment that allows you to move beyond your boundaries and find new possibilities. Make the necessary *Trades* and *Crossovers* and accept both your strengths and weaknesses along the way. There will be failure and of course there will be adjustments, life is just that way, but stay the course, learn from your experiences, remain focused and agile, and you will get there one day. Be sure to manage your time: it is a precious gift, one that we have so little of. Whatever your age, you only have so many Summers. Make your Twenty One rich and fill them with the things that bring you joy, and always remember, *Let Life Treat You Well.* It will if you let it.

Follow us, for book signings, talks, workshops, and
Twenty One Summers community building online and off!

Instagram
@YourTwentyOneSummers
@Twenty.One.Summers

YouTube
@Chasingbeautypublishing

Podcast
Thomas Werner Projects/Twenty One Summers Podcast

Thomas
Instagram @Thomaswernerprojects

Derrick
Instagram @derrick_connell

www.chasingbeautypublishing.com

Notes